John Mackie

Sinners Twain

A Romance of the Great Lone Land

John Mackie

Sinners Twain
A Romance of the Great Lone Land

ISBN/EAN: 9783744673945

Printed in Europe, USA, Canada, Australia, Japan

Cover: Foto ©Thomas Meinert / pixelio.de

More available books at **www.hansebooks.com**

SINNERS TWAIN

A Romance of

THE GREAT LONE LAND

BY

JOHN MACKIE

AUTHOR OF "THE DEVIL'S PLAYGROUND"

London

T. FISHER UNWIN

PATERNOSTER SQUARE

MDCCCXCV

CONTENTS.

CHAP.		PAGE
I.	THE GIRL AND THE SMUGGLER	9
II.	A NORTH-WEST MOUNTED POLICE PARTY	26
III.	"A CAD OF THE FIRST WATER!"	38
IV.	"WILL YOU DO AS I WANT YOU?"	48
V.	HER MANY MOODS	65
VI.	HIS DEAD SELF	74
VII.	AN UNCONSCIOUS PRECEPTOR	87
VIII.	"AN UNCOMMONLY BADLY FROZEN EAR"	98
IX.	WHAT A GIRL WILL DO	112
X.	A TERRIBLE TIME	120
XI.	"GET ON HER TRAIL, PIERRE"	138
XII.	A PURSUIT, A CAPTURE, AND A SURPRISE	155
XIII.	THE PULMAN AND THE SNOW-CLAD PRAIRIE	179
XIV.	IN WHICH THE PRECOCIOUS PRIVATE GETS EVEN WITH THE SERGEANT AND THE SCOUT	191
XV.	A UNIQUE ORDERLY-ROOM SCENE	205
XVI.	SOME LIVES FROM THE RANKS	221
XVII.	OVERHEARD BY THE OLD CROW	233

SINNERS TWAIN.

CHAPTER I.

SHE was a prairie flower, truly, although there were some who would have called her a rare exotic. For the climate of the Canadian North-West is not particularly conducive to female loveliness: it is healthful but trying: the sun's dry passionate kiss in summer, and the Ice-king's breath in winter, have a tendency to roughen and rob the fairest and softest cheek of its bloom. But then, perhaps, on this the south-western slope of the Cypress Hills, just across from the Sweet Grass Hills in Montana, and towards the foot-hills of the Rockies, a little more immunity from such ravages is granted. For here, on the illimitable stretches of coullee-scarred prairie, the soft warm winds from the Pacific Ocean find their way, having wandered through the passes of the Rocky

Mountains, to temper the chill breath of the frozen
North. There is no mystery about these Chinook
winds ; they come from sleeping southern seas where
perpetual summer reigns ; no wonder before their
breath the snow melts like magic. But still the
Red man, in this quarter of the Great Lone Land,
regards them with a superstitious awe. However, it is
only because their influence possibly kept Marie St.
Denis' complexion—which was as pure and velvety
as the skin of a peach—from withering, that these
Chinook winds are mentioned at all.

She leant against the doorway of the long, rambling log house, with its sod roof, ornamented by in-
numerable elk antlers, and watched her father as he
converted a wand of willow into a hoop on which he
meant to stretch the skin of a beaver. But before
we describe the daughter—an excusable tendency—
it would be as well to say a few words about the
father—age before beauty is only justice. He was a
widower, middle-aged, of good physique, and with a
pleasing expression on his face ; his long hair was,
perhaps, prematurely grey, and his skin was tanned
by the sun and wind until it was brown as a berry.
His figure was not an unpicturesque one, suggesting,
as it did, that of the old French trapper or voyageur.
He wore an unplucked beaver cap, a buckskin shirt
flowered and fringed, and a pair of high-heeled
cowboy boots of the orthodox pattern. He was
a typical old-timer ; he was hunter, trapper, and

rancher. In fact, like most men in that country where a picturesque past is fast vanishing, he was anything that would enable him to earn a few dollars, and here, perhaps, lay the mischief. For, mark! these were the days of Prohibition (only in '92 it ceased to exist) in the Territories, and rumour had it that Gabriel St. Denis was not above running a cargo of liquor from across the lines into Canada on an odd occasion. It was a paying, if a wrong, thing to do; besides, there was an indisputable sentiment amongst many that there was no disgrace in so doing; indeed, Gabriel was continually telling himself that what might be a crime need not necessarily be a sin. The anti-Prohibitionists said that the laws prohibiting liquor in the country were made for a time when there were ten Indians to every white man; but now that state of affairs was reversed. Why, they said, should the white population be saddled with a law that was meant for Indians, who were now in a minority? Gabriel did not smuggle liquor for Indians, nor yet retail it. Neither did he introduce into Her Majesty's Dominion what was often felicitously termed "forty-rod," "coffin-varnish," or "tanglefoot," but sound, wholesome rye whiskey. The country was crying out against the abuses that the law engendered; the Mounted Police, and the very judges of the land, found it difficult to reconcile their real sentimehts regarding Prohibition, and what was to them their evident straight course of duty. It was wonderful, however, how elastic the interpretation of the law had become—gutta-percha or india-rubber was nowhere compared to it. There is a case on record when the judge on the bench, while trying a whiskey-smuggling case, said: " I have known the accused for a very long time now, and he is a very decent fellow ; he is not responsible for what his servants do ; therefore I dismiss the case," or words to that effect. Then there was an adjournment for refreshments—of a prohibited nature—in which all parties interested participated, the judge, the accused, and the Mounted Police themselves. They were all jolly good fellows, especially the accused. But let us get back to an infinitely more interesting subject— the girl.

Marie, as has been said, was watching her father as he tied the ends of the long willow wand together. The house was situated just on the edge of a thick clump of cotton-wood trees, and just where the coullee ran out into the prairie. It was well sheltered from the north, east, and west winds. A creek flowed feebly past, and there was a large corral and garden on either side. It was, altogether, a snug and beautiful little spot. One could appreciate such a haven when the blizzards were raging, or when, in the deathly stillness of the long winter nights, the thermometer registered from 10° to 30° below zero ; when the snow-obliterated creek was a solid-channel of ice, and when the intense coldness was a deadly, palpable thing—a thing that caught one's breath and froze it as it issued from the lips.

Upon the girl's face there was a strangely uneasy look, while her eyes seemed to follow the course of Many Berries Creek as, fringed and marked with a straggling growth of trees, it zig-zagged and wandered away over the far-stretching and sun-dried prairie, until it was lost in the misty and uncertain distance. Then her eyes rested on the three peaks of the Sweet Grass Hills that loomed up from their opaline setting like volcanic islands surrounded by a vaporous, shipless sea; and, figuratively, in this wild region they were islands, for between them and Gabriel St. Denis' house (only a year or two ago) there was no human life, only, perhaps, a small band of wandering Blood, Sioux or Piegan Indians on the hunt, or some less innocent amusement.

She was a truly remarkable looking girl this daughter of Gabriel's, for there never were two people who could agree as to the colour of her eyes or hair. Some said her eyes were hazel, some said blue, and some said brown. The truth was, they seemed to change colour with every mood that showed on her mobile face. There was always a limpid depth in them, which, with the fresh colour of her face, and her red lips, indicated a healthful, buoyant nature. Her hair was, indeed, of that colour which Georgione and Titian gave to their Venetian women, "brown in the shade, golden in the sun."

Her figure was finely moulded, and, perhaps, the dead plainness and flowing lines of her neat dress only showed it to a better advantage. Her shapely, proud head was well poised upon that beautifully rounded neck which sculptors love to create—for, alas, it is so seldom found. But she was, perhaps, a girl no longer, for she stood on the mystic threshold of womanhood, and there was that inscrutable look in her eyes as of one who listens. From her small hands and feet, to her dimpled, resolute chin and low, broad forehead, there was no tame or commonplace feature. Had she lived in London, or Paris, or any other great city, artists would have discovered her, have made her famous, and worshipped her; and women would have paid her truer homage still, for they would have said all manner of false and spiteful things regarding her, and have heartily hated her. But she was only "that girl of old St. Denis'," who lived like a recluse some twenty miles distant from his nearest neighbour on the prairie of the Canadian North-West. She was an anomaly: like a golden room in a wooden house. She ought to have been without a heartache (how much after all does a man know about that complex thing a woman's heart?); but, as it was, the girl dreamed her dreams, and wove the romances of a coming womanhood amid what seemed such uncongenial surroundings for a bright young life. Perhaps, that subtle spirit of solitude which settles down over that great lone prairie land with the blood-red sunsets, had tinged her with somewhat of that pensiveness which occasionally seemed to haunt her face.

And now Gabriel spoke, in a somewhat embarrassed manner it must be confessed ; he did not look up at the pretty picture before him, but wound another piece of string round the joint of the hoop—a quite unnecessary thing to do—with an apparent concentration of purpose that was utterly wasted.

" Oh, by the way, little un', I was nigh forgettin' to tell ye, that I'll be gwin away for a week or ten days to Benton to git some necess'ries I can't git y'ere. I s'pose, now, ye won't mind bein' left alone for thet time ? You've got old Jeannette, you know, and I'll fetch you a present from Benton—some of these yere books ye can't git on this side without givin' ever so much for —— "

" Oh, Dad ! "

It was almost like the cry of a wounded animal ; but still she did not withdraw her eyes from the vague, blue line of the uneven horizon : only, all at once, the light had gone out of them, and there was an apprehensive, piteous look there instead. She had clasped her hands together in front of her involuntarily, and then, as if ashamed at having been betrayed even into this momentary expression of feeling, she caught at and plucked nervously the leaves of some creeping plant that clambered up the doorway of the house. It could be easily seen that she felt ashamed and humiliated by what she had to say to her father. There was a momentary twitching of her lips, then a droop about the corners of her mouth ; but she recovered herself in another minute with a visible effort, and continued—

"Dad, didn't you tell me that you would not go across there any more ? Cannot we live without your having to go there ? Some day the Mounted Police will be running across you as you come back, and not only take your horses and waggons, but will fine you besides ever so many hundreds of dollars, and then what will you have gained in the end ? Oh, Dad," and there was a world of entreaty and self-deprecation in that soft voice of hers, "it is not for me to preach to you, but if you only knew how miserable this thing makes me I don't think you would do it. Besides, how do you think—though I don't care so much about myself after all—I can go into Medicine Hat, and hold up my head, knowing that everybody is pointing to me and saying, 'There goes Marie St. Denis, the ——.' " But she only bit her lips and left unfinished what she had begun.

"There's hardly a soul in the 'Hat,' barring the parsons," interrupted Gabriel, hotly, but somewhat shamefacedly it must be confessed, and without lifting his head, "thinks any the worse of a man for bein' in th' whiskey bizness. No one thinks any-thin' about it ; and the jedges ain't so very hard upon a man for smugglin' now. I believe if there was license in the country there'd be less hypocrisy an' hard drinkin'—it's a foolish law—an injuist law."

"But it's the law," she persisted, "and I can't bear to see you break it. I am sure we can manage to live without you doing this thing. My wants are not many, and they can be made fewer. You need not take me into Medicine Hat this winter; and I have lots of good clothes. You know I can make lots of money if you will let me. Look at all those moccasins I have made, and sewed with silk and beadwork, and those beaver caps and mitts. There are shops in town would only be too glad to get them, and I could work lots more. I am sure there is no necessity for you to run any risks for my sake."

And now there was a pleading, wistful look in her eyes as she spoke; there was entreaty in every delicate feature of her face; there was a suppressed pathos in her soft and modulated voice.

As her name denoted, she was of French descent on her father's side, but her mother had been a Scotswoman. Perhaps it was to this fact that the girl owed somewhat of her complex nature, that quick, sympathetic turn of mind : the lively imagination and light-heartedness of the French, alongside the deep-rooted religious instincts and stable, thoughtful nature of the Scotch. Though Gabriel could talk French—and Marie, too, for the matter of that—there was nothing in their speech that would have

2

led a stranger to suppose so. Gabriel's father, when
the former was a mere child, had left the French
settlements and pushed out West, and circumstances
having thrown the son nearly all his life amongst the
English-speaking population, he had contracted that
nondescript form of speech peculiar to the Western
man and the frontiersman.

Gabriel surreptitiously unloosed the double string
that converted the willow into a hoop, and made a
show of being annoyed as the ends flew asunder.
That he was uneasy, and fighting out a battle within
himself, there could be little doubt. He nerved himself, however, and laughed in a hard, brusque way,
very unlike his real self, as he replied—

"'Ough! Ough!' as the Niche says, and what
nonsense is it talking about now, 'bout working
moccasin, fur caps, and mitts, just as if it were a
squaw or a breed, and hevin' to sell them, too. Now,
look 'e y'ere, Marie. I don't 'xactly know what I've
bin doin' to put sich notions in yere head ; I'm sure
you's allus had all the money you's iver wanted to.
In fact, I kin hardly iver git ye to tek any. Why,
my child, instead of bein' a beggar, as ye seem to
think, I've a matter of ten thousan' dollars laid by,
an' only want to mek a little more so's to help us
leave this played-out country—for since the buffalo's
gone I've no more use for it—an' then we'll strike the
trail an' go 'way down south into Uncle Sam's
country, and tek some nice farm where ye'll hev lots

o' comp'ny, and won't be boxed up yere as ye're now. I've bin thinkin' of late it's hardly the spryest kin' o' life for a young gal."

Poor man, it had hardly dawned upon him that she was now no longer a "young gal." He loved her with all the silent and conserved force of an un-demonstrative nature, and, perhaps, love is slow to observe change. And then, her mother having died when she was but a child, and Gabriel having wisely sent her to the convent at Prince Albert, on the Saskatchewan, to be educated, he had, doubtless, seen too little of her. He was a good-hearted man, and considering the nomadic, frontier life he had led as trapper and buffalo hunter in the far West, since he had left his old home in Ontario, and since the death of his wife, was doubtless an exemplary man as com-pared with most of his kind. When he had taken his daughter from the convent of Prince Albert he had honestly intended to do his duty by his child, and so he had, according to his own lights. He had taken her some forty miles south of the Canadian Pacific Railway, to the south-western slope of the Cypress Hills, into this lonely but beautiful country, and started a ranche. But his progress in acquiring what his heart was set upon, a sufficient sum of money to take up a good improved farm in one of the settled and sunny Southern States, was slow ; and then the temptation to make money easily and quickly pre-sented itself. It was by running cargoes of liquor into Canada from across the lines. In other words, by smuggling. For a long time he resisted the temptation; but when he found how public sentiment ran, and that the law prohibiting liquor was looked upon by many as an iniquitous one, he regarded the project with less disfavour. "He who doubts is doomed" may apply to various phases of moral philosophy. "It is all for Marie," he said to himself; rather illogically, it must be confessed, and to conciliate his by no means dormant moral sense. And surely the girl was too young to associate any very serious breach of morality with such proceedings. His first few ventures were successful, and paid him well. He began to think, with many in the North-West, that thus to contravene the law was neither a sin nor a crime. Then, later on, it became not so much a matter of conscience with him as his daughter's peace of mind; for, of course, he could not expect to keep such a traffic concealed from her; but up till now she had not seemed to take it so very seriously. He had acquired what to many in that country was wealth, but he wanted just another five or six hundred dollars and then he would quit the trade, and "strike the trail," as he termed it. There was no other woman within twenty miles of them save the old French half-breed, Jeannette, who assisted in the household duties, and, truly, she was a never-failing source of entertainment. For in the long winter nights when King Frost held everything in his deadly grip outside, and the stove hummed with a cheery sound, many were the wonderful legends and tales told of the days when the old French voyageurs penetrated far into the heart of the great Unknown with their canoes ; of the battles with the Indians ; of the solemn councils ; of the immense herds of buffalo that stretched from horizon to horizon, and a hundred picturesque features of the Great Lone Land now fast passing away. Indeed, Marie was an exemplary daughter, and never once complained of dulness. The height of her dissipation was occasionally accompanying her father into Medicine Hat, or " The Hat," as this remarkable example in nomenclature was termed, and to skate with the little crowd on the Saskatchewan of an afternoon, or to have a glimpse of those wonderful cars, which stopped there for half an hour, on that great world's highway, the Canadian Pacific Railway, with their wonderfully assorted loads of human beings. Her wants were few and simple ; she was content when she saw her father attending to his more legitimate duties, and looking happy and contented.

Perhaps Gabriel was troubled with a consciousness that he had not altogether done his duty by her. Anyhow, he had never heard her express herself so strongly as she did now.

" Why, Marie," he ventured at length, and without looking up, " what has made ye become so perticklar

all of a suddin? I remimbers the time when ye used
to laugh when ye he'rd of the way we'd give the p'lice
the slip." Then he continued in a somewhat lower
tone, and not without a certain twinkle in his eye,
"And p'rhaps some o' th' p'lice themsel's 'er not so
very perticklar as to whether they catch us or not—
surely that sergeant, who comes over now an' agen
from Willow Creek, has not bin putin' eny nonsense
into yer head?"

To do the man justice, as has been said he only
looked upon her as a child, and did not dream for an
instant that what he said would have the slightest
significance for her. He was tying the end of the
hoop together again, and did not see her face as he
spoke. She had started slightly, and, indeed, her
face had paled for an instant before the warm blood
had mounted into it. Her lips had closed on each
other, and her eyes had looked fixedly away down
the creek bottom as if they were watching the
flight of a covey of prairie chickens. At length she
spoke.

"I hardly understand you, dad, when you talk
about some one putting nonsense into my head.
You forget the sergeant is a gentleman, and it was
not difficult to see that last time he was here he
meant well by you, for, you remember, he mentioned,
as if by accident, something about that extra patrol
along the boundary line which they had begun. It
wasn't difficult to see he felt miserably ill at ease

lest we should guess the motives that led him to speak of it. For, of course, he meant it as a warning to you, which few men would have done, otherwise he would have told you in a very different fashion. As for the corruption—there is only one name for it—you hint at, I am sure he is above anything like that."

And now that maidenly spirit of reserve, as she spoke, had entirely left her; she held her head almost proudly, and there was a fuller touch of colour in her cheek. There was that air of nobility about her that glorifies a beautiful woman when she is championing the absent. Not that the absent was anything to her : for loyalty in a noble-minded woman is a comprehensive and catholic virtue.

"Yes, Marie," said Gabriel, who still did not seem to notice her aroused interest, " I dropped as to how 'e meant it. He's a chap as'll do his duty, an' I gives him credit for thet same, and I'll give him a wide berth. But there's Jeannette. Now I'se jist a goin' to run th' horses into th' c'ral, for it'll soon be dark. I hope it won't snow afore I git back, but it's gettin' late in the Fall. I must start to-morrow, honey. I guess I'll be back in less'n ten days' time. I'll just give ye a call on my way back to the Hat and see thet ye're all snug. The p'lice were yere on Monday, so I don' s'pose they'll be back for 'nother fortnight, an' by thet time I'll be yere agen. Come, Marie," and, suddenly throwing away the hoop, he put his arm round her and drew her into the house. Then he reappeared with his bridle over his arm to fetch the horses up. He had been anxious to put an end to the conversation ; it was a much. more unpleasant one for him than he had cared to admit.

And now the profound and solemn stillness that broods over that vast and lonely rolling prairie seemed to deepen. The prairie chickens and other birds had drunk at the feebly flowing creek, and had gone back to the sheltering edge of the scrub for the night. The great cinnamon bear which at this season of the year leaves the sheltering pine forests, and wanders down the coullee and creek bottoms to fossick out roots, and feast on the luscious wild berries, rose from his lair amid the thick, long grass and thicker undergrowth, and came boldly out on to the bare hillside to have a look around. A keen black frost set in ; one could hear the crackle of the growing covering of ice on the beaver dam, and the more startling rending of the dead cotton-wood trees up the coullee as Jack Frost squeezed them in his icy grip. The stars gleamed out more sharply and clearly in the dusk of the heavens, and towards the Arctic circle the Aurora-Borealis, that " Dance of the Spirits " as the Indians call it, suddenly burst into life and light, its quivering shafts of pearly and silvery fire darting from one side to another, crossing and recrossing : creating a living halo and glory around the throne of the great Ice-king. Now the log house and other buildings showed black as jet against it. From the little uncurtained windows poured mellow streams of light into the cold, crisp air, and showed right cheerily indeed. It was a cozy and pretty picture truly, this tiny speck of civilisation in the lonely wilderness, when these unwinking eyes of fire looked out boldly into the gloom, as if rejoicing over the fuller life within.

CHAPTER II.

TEN days after the conversation narrated in the preceding chapter, and about a couple of miles or so above St. Denis' ranche, up the coullee, four men are grouped together under a peculiarly formed water-worn cliff of yellow sandstone. They are seated in what was once the bed of the creek. But that prince of engineers, the beaver, had constructed a large dam just above them, and diverted the course of the stream. In Canada, beavers sometimes convert meadows into lakes, swamp homesteads, change the course of all-important creeks, and it is no uncommon sight to see a bridge left high and dry, like some stranded leviathan, rendered quite unnecessary by these arch practical jokers.

The most important individual in the party referred to, not only in his own eyes, but by virtue of rank, was a commissioned officer of Mounted Police. His eyes were dark, and his whole facial expression might be summed up in three words—red, round, and vulgar.

Indeed, he enjoyed the sobriquet of "Pudding-face Jamie," from the supposed resemblance of the facial features aforesaid to that popular but homely article of diet. He had at one time been a private holding some subordinate "staff job" in the force, but, having the necessary influence at his back, had secured a commission. Those of his old chums in the force, who had expected that when Jamie became an officer he would at least have some consideration for his old comrades, were grievously disappointed ; for, true to the old adage regarding the putting of a beggar on horseback, when he tasted power he rode rough-shod over the unfortunates under him. Fortunately, most of his brother officers (the exception being those drawn from his own substratum of society) were gentlemen by birth and education, splendid all-round, good-hearted fellows as one could wish to meet, so they, providentially, kept such characters as Jamie in check, and saved many a gently-nurtured youth from a martyrdom of petty but galling annoyances. For in the Mounted Police a few years ago, a very large percentage of the men belonging to the rank and file were gentlemen. Of course Jamie resented the presence of gentlemen: they offered too great a contrast to his own condition—a condition which not even a gold crown on the collar of his serge, and goodness knows how many yards of gold lace besides, could ever ameliorate. This was where the shoe pinched with Jamie. No wonder that the milk of

human kindness was somewhat soured in his composition. The three others present were a police
sergeant, a private, and a French quarter-breed scout
named Pierre, a short, stout, dark-eyed and pleasant-
looking individual upon the whole. He had a weak-
ness for saying what were meant to be funny things,
while at the same time his face bore a look of preternatural gravity. But just then the fact of Jamie
having only informed him that he would recommend
the Commissioner to discharge him on the completion
of the trip, had somewhat damped Pierre's natural
cheerfulness. The sergeant was a smart, dark, hand-
some-looking fellow, and like many more in his
position seemed born for better things. Even now
although his face was unshaven, although the stump
of an old briar pipe protruded from between his lips,
and his seedy old buffalo coat was buttoned up to his
chin, one could see at a glance that Harry Yorke was
a gentleman. The fourth man of the party seemed
rather a young individual to be a policeman. He was
the son of a younger son—some army officer with a
large family and limited means who was only too
glad to get one of his boys disposed of, even if it were
in the ranks of the North-West Mounted Police; for
then the youth would be self-supporting and would
give no further trouble. As it was, Dick Townley,
like many more young men in a like position, found
the life was not exactly a bed of roses—when, for
instance, an officer like Jamie ordered him while in

the post to gather bones in a gunny-sack, round the Barrack Square, which had been deposited there by other people's dogs, or remove the refuse in the spring from behind the officers' quarters, in close proximity to an Indian who was ornamented with a ball and chain attached to one leg. Doubtless, so far as the Indian was concerned, the punishment was not undeserved, for he had, probably, got six months for appropriating another Indian's squaw, and breaking the former's head when politely remonstrated with. As for the unfortunate private—well, somebody had to do the scavenger's work. It was not, perhaps, then to be wondered at that his speech partook of a certain cynical and sarcastic tone when the conversation referred to his superior officer. Indeed, it might be almost said to savour of disloyalty; but then, in the often circumscribed and lonely life of the trooper, there were things said, done, and tolerated, that would not have been dreamt of under different conditions. In the ranks of the Mounted Police, partly on account of that subtle affinity of class, and conscious necessity of mutual help and encouragement in a life which is to a certain extent one of exile, there was a healthful spirit of *camaraderie*, the like of which, perhaps, does not exist in any other force of the kind in the world. Between the non-commissioned officers and privates there was a mutual understanding and good feeling, that made the duties of the former comparatively easy and pleasant. Perhaps it was this spirit that made the sergeant tolerant and take no notice of his junior's many colloquial divergencies.

There were six saddle and pack horses, hard by, in a little clump of bushes. Only a few bleached or blackened leaves clung in a forlorn looking fashion, like tattered signals of distress, to the great gaunt trees and the dense undergrowth. On three sides they were so hemmed in by trees that they could hardly see the opposite bank of the coullee, although, straight across, it could hardly be more than a couple of hundred yards or so. It was bitterly cold, and the party sat moodily, muffled up in their buffalo coats ; their saddles and gear were lying about. They had made a fire, over which they hung, and its effect was cheerful enough despite the dispiriting social atmosphere just then. The wood they burned was old, and of such a nature that the little smoke from it could hardly attract attention. And now the sky had become overcast, and they knew that high above heads, up on the "bench," or plateau, a light breeze had sprung up. At last the scout spoke, the volatile little man could contain himself no longer, even although he had just as good as "got the sack."

"*Parbleu !*" he exclaimed. "It is not surprised I should be if we were going to have just a leetle snow-storm. Generally it is we have one before this time of the year. A-ha, *mon cher* Richard, and how it is you will love the entertainment of a snow blanket ?"

"Why, my well-beloved Sancho," answered the youthful private addressed, " that is a most delightful contingency to contemplate. It reminds me of a legend somewhere, an Indian eda, a Grecian myth, a Scandinavian saga, or something of that sort "— here he glanced furtively at his superior officer—" or is it taken from ' The Pilgrim's Progress ' or ' Robinson Crusoe '? No matter ; but it is about two small children who, persecuted by a wicked uncle, were lost in a great wood, and the robins, and moas, tom-tits and dodos came and covered them up with leaves. Now, Pierre, I think you would make a most beautiful and interesting babe all covered up with leaves, or saddle-blankets, or supposing this cliff were suddenly to cave in—with rocks."

" Eh ! what saire ? " exclaimed the little scout with a merry twinkle in his eye at this stage of the extravaganza. He had not exactly followed it, but he knew that the private was trying to make fun of him.

" By the jumping Gewhitaker ! " broke in the bearer of the Queen's commission who had been silently wondering if what the private had been talking about were really some " classical stuff," or nonsense specially concocted to annoy him. " I wish you two fools would hold your tongues. Get both of you away up to the bench, and come back and tell me what you see there—take the field-glasses with you."

" Very good, sir," said the trooper, picking up the

glasses which Jamie had indicated by glancing one of his bulging eyes in their direction, and moving off. But the little scout still lingered with an inquiring expression on his face.

"Well, what in the devil's name are you waiting for now, eh?" inquired Jamie. "Sergeant, I call you to witness this fellow's rank insubordination." Jamie was almost cheerful now, for he never felt so happy as when putting a charge for some breach of discipline against a newly-made corporal, or badgering some willing but not over quick-witted constable.

"Please, saire, shall I my horse take?" inquired the scout, with a look of preternatural gravity on his face, and as an interpretation of his conduct.

"No, you fool; take these drum-stick legs of yours. You grow stupider every day, Pierre."

Pierre smiled pleasantly as he turned his back, as if he had just been complimented. And so he had—when he could make Jamie believe that he was growing stupider.

In a few minutes the pair were back in camp again.

"Well?" inquired the Amiable One before either of them had time to speak. "Have both of you lost your tongues?"

The scout, unseen to the officer, stuck his into his left cheek so that the constable might see it, and answered—

"There is nothing, saire, to be seen. But I think

we will have a snow-storm, and it is snowed-in we are liable to be, if we remain here."

"And who in the name of all that's wonderful " (only he put it a little more forcibly) " told you that we were going to remain here?" asked Jamie, grimly rejoicing in the opportunity afforded of making things lively generally. " Darn you, Pierré! I wish you would give a straightforward answer to a straightforward question. I don't want you to make suggestions; you are not paid for that. It is not necessary for you to point out anything. Sergeant, you and Townley get a rustle on, and saddle up the horses; we'll make for shelter."

And now a few flakes of snow began to fall, undecidedly and reluctantly. Then they came down faster and faster, as if at last they saw there was no help for it and might as well do the business with credit to themselves when they were at it. In a few minutes more, something like a blizzard had developed with all the suddenness which dwellers in these latitudes have at times experienced.

But before this happened the sergeant and the private had gone off to fetch up the horses; the scout had picked up a heavy Mexican bridle, and, with a significant light in his protruding eyes, addressed the officer. The latter, when he had seen that the scout was about to address him, had preluded the communication with, " Well, what are you going to interfere with now?"

Slowly, deliberately, and with evident unction, Pierre spoke.

"Saire, I do not wish to interfere or to point out anything, but I would respectfully suggest that the pair of spare beaver mitts belonging to you and lying on that burning log be removed. Already they are *en partie* consumed—I hope you will pardon me for pointing out——"

He was not allowed to finish the sentence, for the officer sprang forward with an oath and rescued the mitts from further destruction. To do the scout justice, he had not observed the smouldering mitts until it was too late to save them. And now Jamie had something tangible to work upon to gratify his passion for fault-finding, and he let loose on the head of the scout a torrent of abuse that would have done credit to a gamin from the slums of Whitechapel, or a Queensland bullock-driver. But Pierre paid no heed, and consoled himself with the thought that a new pair of mitts would cost Jamie at least three dollars, and that would go pretty near to breaking his heart.

And now they were ready for a start.

"Where to, sir?" inquired the sergeant.

"Why, to old St. Denis', to be sure! Where else?" asked the officer, impatiently.

"Well, sir, it's only a matter of ten miles if we make over to Willow Creek through Wild-cat coullee, and we can intercept St. Denis' party just as easily from there. If we go to his house we may miss him altogether."

"No, I guess we will go and stop at old St. Denis' until that gentleman comes back," said the Amiable One, as Dick Townley, the private, in a spirit of mild irony, had dubbed him.

Now, if the sergeant had only exercised a little forethought, and had proposed to go to St. Denis' in the first place, his superior officer would have promptly vetoed it, and have ordered him to proceed somewhere else. The Scriptures characterise such a spirit as "stiff-neckedness," but in the States they have improved upon the expression, and call it "pure cussedness." Jamie continued, after a brief pause—

"Besides, Gabriel's sure to look in just to see how that rather smartish girl of his is getting on, on his way to the Hat ; and then we can nab him and the liquor too—savey ?"

The sergeant looked at his superior with not a little ill-concealed disgust upon his face as he replied—

"But excuse me, sir ; he's not likely to fetch the liquor there ; and you forget that there are only two women left at St. Denis', and in a small place like that there's hardly room for us. I don't see that we have any right to take possession of a man's house because he happens to be away, even although he is suspected of smuggling—more especially when he has only left two defenceless women to protect it. Of course, if you intend going into some outhouse it won't matter so much."

" Outhouse, be d——d ! " exclaimed Jamie, impatiently, and with a look of superior wisdom. " I say, Yorke, you've got to see a little more of life and the world yet before you can get along in this country."

A wise man, if he has not travelled, is as worthy of respect as the thoughtful man who has, in that he realises his own littleness and paves the way to knowledge. But a fool is like a fat donkey that ventures upon thin ice : he courts extinction by the weight of his own ignorance.

The sergeant had turned quickly when Jamie spoke, and looked full in the face of his superior officer with not a little surprise, then considerable amusement. As he went slowly on without making any reply, a pitying smile crossed his features as he ejaculated under his breath, " Poor devil ! "

" Harry," said the private, to his older comrade the sergeant, as the scout and Jamie headed down the coullee, and with a look of mock gravity on his face, " don't you wish you had seen as much life as the Amiable One ? "

" Come, now," answered the sergeant, " none of your treasonable remarks—let's talk of something else. By Jove, though, I can't help wishing that old fool St. Denis had stayed at home ! If it weren't for that poor girl of his, I'd say serve him right to get caught—and ten chances to one we'll nab him this time. It's a shame of him to ruin her life like this —and she is such a superior sort of girl ; I think her mother must have been a decided cut above the common run of them, though old Gabriel's not such an unpresentable looking old fellow himself. And by the way, Dick, I don't suppose you've seen her yet. It won't do, you know, to get soft upon her."

" Ah ! I see—soft yourself, eh ? " said Dick, disrespectfully.

" Well, not quite," was the answer, in a tone that did not exactly reassure the youngster, and still less invited further discussion of the subject.

CHAPTER III.

"A CAD OF THE FIRST WATER!"

SHE stood outside the house, bareheaded, and looked towards the sky, while her hands were outstretched in front of her, palms upward. The light breeze caught up the silky wealth of gleaming hair that had escaped from its heavy folds for the time being, until it streamed in mid-air behind her like a shimmering shaft of golden light : it kissed and heightened the delicate colour on her cheek. A few feathery flakes of snow melted away as they fell upon her firm white palms : even if they had been animate things, perhaps, they would have been quite content to pass away there. There was a look of concern upon Marie St. Denis' face as she looked all around before going into the house again.

"Jeannette," she said to an elderly and tidy-looking French half-breed woman, "I believe we are going to have a storm. Oh, I hope dad is in some safe place ! It makes me ill to think of him being on the prairie, and perhaps a bad blizzard coming on."

"He'll be all right, *ma cherie;* fret not yourself," said old Jeannette, cheerily. But she said under her breath all the same, "and serve him right for going, the wicked man!"

It was a long, low room, and scrupulously clean. To use a rather absurd but popular saying, "you might have eaten your dinner off the floor" (just as if there was any necessity for any one to perpetrate such an inconvenient and barbarous deed!), so beautifully clean and fresh it was. There were some humble and not unsuccessful attempts at adornment in this room. For into each of the windows were fitted little boxes, in which still bloomed some hardy plants. There was an absence of all cheap or gaudy ornamentation, which is so often found in the houses of those whose love of show is paramount to their love of the beautiful. But there were some unique and not unbeautiful specimens of wrought Indian bead-work hung against the wall that made one think of the time when interiors were hung with tapestry. One end of the room was sacred to the burnished and well-kept culinary articles of Jeannette. Here and there against the walls, mounted fan-shape, were white owls with their feathers like great ruffles surrounding their beautiful heads; and eagle-hawks, fierce and picturesque, mounted in a like fashion. They were a species of ornamentation that any drawing-room in Belgravia might have been proud of.

Unconsciously in keeping with a prevailing fashion

stood a small triangular glass-fronted cupboard, with
some wonderful old china in it, in one corner of the
room.   That china had belonged to the girl's mother
and grandmother, and was a sacred thing.   There
was a pair of brass-mounted, flint-lock pistols crossed
over a quaint, narrow, and high mirror, and beautiful
stone Indian tomahawks and pipes, whose helves and
stems were a rich mosaic of coloured beads and from
which dangled eagles' feathers.   Crossed over this
doorway was a pair of snowshoes, and over that one,
in the centre, was a magnificent elk's head, whose
antlers touched the ceiling.   And there were two
tiny models of birch-bark canoes, and Indian rowers
in them with paddles poised in air.   On a small table
at the far end of the room there was a unique grass-
like woven cloth that was made beautiful and striking
by having a fantastic pattern wrought on it in
coloured silks and beads, and heavily fringed.   The
yellow and red colours which the Crees affect pre-
dominated in it.   Strange it is to think—and few
there are, perhaps, who know it—that the Crees got
these colours from the Mexicans, when the former
were a bold and warlike race—when their territory
lay far to the south, and ere they were driven
gradually backwards by younger and stronger races.
Though there was a certain air of barbaric splendour
about that cloth, still the effect of the whole room
was in keeping with, and characteristic of, those
romantic and picturesque elements of a past now

vanishing before a more prosaic nineteenth-century utilitarianism. There was, indeed, really good taste displayed in the arrangement of every detail in that room. Not even the conventional cooking and box-stove and lengths of piping could detract from the quaintness of that old-world interior, for they were blackened and polished till they reflected one's image like a mirror.

Then the girl put an iron on the stove, and looked at a little heap of collars and cuffs which lay upon the dresser ready to be operated upon.

"Sit down, Jeannette," she said, "and tell me a story while I iron these things—something about the old French voyageurs, or about the early days of Fort Garry before Riel came to make the *metis* dissatisfied."

Just at this moment a great wiry-haired dog, something between a Scotch staghound and a sheep-dog, lifted its head and growled ominously. It had been lying half asleep in front of the stove. The girl started significantly and placed one finger against her lower lip. The half-breed woman put her head on one side and listened intently. Then they heard the dull, uneven thud of horses' feet, and dark shadows, as it were, passed and momentarily darkened the front windows. In another minute there was a loud, irregular knocking at the door; then it was thrown open, and a great fur-clad figure stumbled into the room, powdered with snow.

"What a devil of a day!" it exclaimed.

It is perhaps unnecessary to say this was the gentleman, already referred to, who had the honour of bearing Her Majesty's commission.

In another second another figure entered, but it came no farther than the door, and closed it so as to shut out the drifting snow. This figure was the sergeant, who did not speak, but, indeed, seemed somewhat embarrassed.

The girl still stood as if transfixed with astonishment at this sudden entry, or as if these uninvited guests hailed from another world, instead of being only matter-of-fact Mounted Policemen. But, surely, it was something more than mere astonishment that paled her cheek, and for a second made her lean against the dresser as if for support. Who can tell what thoughts passed through that poor girl's mind just then? It was not difficult to speculate upon one all-powerful vision that rose up before her, and that was her father. Into her expressive, wide-open eyes there came a look of startled apprehension, and then the consciousness of some dreaded presence, which was pitiful to look upon in one so young. But the gallant leader of the party called back the colour into her cheeks. The inspector was a married man, but he possessed a way with him which he considered was all-potent with the fair sex. Perhaps it had been potent to a certain extent—in that sphere which he adorned.

"Now then, Mary Ann," he said, "you don't look as if you were glad to see me as I know you are. Just get a rustle on like a dear, and shove another log into that stove and—damn it! take that big, ugly brute away for goodness sake!"

The great hound was growling and sniffing in a suspicious fashion in the neighbourhood of the officer's ankles, occasioning that gentleman no little concern.

"Sh—h— get away, Michelle! Lie down, sirre!" cried Jeannette, catching up a billet of wood and chasing the hound from the visitors, much to Jamie's satisfaction.

And now the claim of strangers to the rites of hospitality had dawned upon the startled girl; and as if she had not heard the officer's free and easy speech, she said—

"Won't you sit down? you must be cold," and she placed chairs for them near the stove, and was handling a fresh log to put in the box-stove, when the sergeant came quickly towards her.

"Allow me, Miss St. Denis," he said.

At the same moment he had drawn off his mitts, and seized the log of wood she had lifted, in both hands. In doing this his hand accidentally touched hers; she looked up at him suddenly, and the colour on her cheek deepened not a little. "How cold your hands are," she remarked; "their touch quite startled me: they are like lead." But she let him take the log ; and, perhaps, he did not know that this simple, common place act of politeness, which with some would have passed as a matter of course, was recognised gratefully by her as a deference she felt was only her due, even if she were only Gabriel St. Denis' daughter.

"Have you put your horses in the stable ? " Marie asked, turning to the sergeant. "There are four or five spare stalls, you know, and lots of hay."

It was significant that she did not address herself to the officer. But Jamie resented this. He must show this untutored child of the prairie that he was in command of the party.

"Don't fret, my dear," he remarked, with an assumption of graceful facetiousness ; "my men know how to make themselves at home. You press the button—I mean, you find the hay, and we do the rest."

Marie looked at him wonderingly for an instant. She did not know whether to put this man's strange speech down to his ignorance of the common civilities of every-day life, or to a chronic crudeness, or rudeness of manner. She only slightly bit her lip, and made no comment. She would be charitable, and ascribe his familiarity to the former hypothesis : it would not do to neglect the sacred rites of hospitality, even if—and here her heart sank within her at the thought.

In another minute the private and the scout had

come into the room. At last, Jamie asked abruptly—

"When do you expect the old man back?"

The sergeant turned uneasily in his chair, when he saw the look of wistful entreaty and pain upon the girl's face on hearing this blunt question.

"If you mean my father," she answered, "I am not in a position to tell you. Do you wish particularly to see him?"

"Yup—yaas, I just reckon we want to—to have an opportunity of interviewing him," answered Jamie in his happiest manner. He was under the impression that his humour was of a light and graceful kind, and he looked into the faces of the others to mark the signs of appreciation of these qualities. But he was nettled at discovering only a stolid imperturbability in them. Had his perceptive faculties not been so dulled by conceit, he might possibly have detected a look of unqualified disgust and shame there instead.

"Now, look here, my dear," he continued, "it's no use of you trying this innocent sort of dodge on with me. We want to see the old man, and I guess we'll see him, s'posin' we've got to wait in this 'ere house for a fortnight——"

"Sir!" interrupted the girl suddenly, and turning her great clear eyes full upon him, with almost an incredulous look in them.

The sergeant coughed and shifted uneasily in his seat. The constable kicked the heel of the scout surreptitiously with his out-stretched foot; and the

latter seemed to find something that interested him
immensely in a pair of snowshoes which were
crossed on the wall over the dresser. The half-
breed woman paused in the performance of some
work, folded her arms, and looked at the officer with
brows that knitted like gathering storms. But Jamie
saw none of these signs and continued—

" You don't seem to understand, my dear; a pretty
girl like you——"

But he had overstepped the mark this time. The
warm blood mounted into the girl's face : she held
her head erect, and looked at him unflinchingly as
she interrupted—

" Sir, by what right do you insult two defenceless
women ? "

The sergeant's breath came and went in quick
gasps. Could he risk calling his superior officer
to a sense of what was proper, and rely on Townley,
the private, and the scout becoming temporarily
deaf? For he knew if he spoke it meant a serious
charge of insurbordination against him. But the
officer himself released his subordinate from his difficulty, and brought about his own undoing. He
stared blankly at her for a moment, as if he had not
rightly heard ; then, realising that his authority—a
high and mighty officer's of the North-West Mounted
Police—had been called in question by a frail girl,
his round moon-like face became flushed and purple
—the change was inconsiderable from its normal

one—as he blurted out in a tone meant to impress the entire party, and overawe this spirited girl in particular—

"Girl, do you know who and what I am ? "

"You have just enlightened us on these points," she answered, in a strangely quiet and subdued manner, "for your actions and a certain reputation are identical."

"Eh—what ? " he asked uneasily ; he had not exactly followed her, but he thought his manner had evidently impressed this wayward girl. "Who and what am I, then ? "

"An officer of the North-West Mounted Police," she replied calmly, "and a cad of the first water ! "

As Pierre (who chuckled to himself for nearly two hours after this speech) said to Dick Townley that night, the girl was, indeed, "a chip of the old block."

CHAPTER IV.

"WILL YOU DO AS I WANT YOU?"

THE sergeant rose to his feet : he could not sit by any longer and be an impassive witness of such a scene. To say that he felt heartily ashamed at this moment of the cloth he wore, and for the well-merited rebuke just accorded it by this beautiful and indignant girl, were putting it mildly.

Jamie sat speechless, with his dark eyes fairly bulging out of his head. That a mere slip of a girl should have the audacity to openly insult him—of course there was no question of insult in so far as his conduct in relation to her was concerned—an officer and a gentleman—oh, of course, a gentleman—and before his subordinates, too—was a thing so un-paralleled in Inspector Jamie Bounder's vast ex-perience (in the Great Lone Land), that it left him literally incapable of thought or action. To use one of his own beautiful and choice expressions, he was "tee-totally flabergasted" for the moment. The private had risen with the sergeant, and made for the door. But the conduct of the little scout was most remarkable, for, on rising, he had, curiously enough, kicked his hat into a corner of the room, and appeared to have considerable difficulty in picking it up again. He reminded one of an ostrich with its head stuck in a hole, and its huge body gravitating aimlessly round it. He—Pierre—however, snorted in a most peculiar and suspicious fashion.

But it was the old half-breed woman who took advantage of the situation to interfere on behalf of her young mistress, and put a check to the uncalled-for impertinences of the gallant officer. Her dark face became sallow; her black, sharp eyes sparkled ominously; her high, quavering voice betrayed her excitable Gallic origin as she faced the somewhat surprised officer, and cried, with a determined stamp of her foot—

"You shall not; I say you shall not, no matter what you are, sit here and insult my young mistress. If you cannot see you are an unwelcome *convié* in this room, you must be asked to relieve us of your presence, and get out of it! We cannot in this storm ask you to leave the house, but there is one large room you can have, it is to the right of the passage as you come in, with a stove in it. You will be good enough to remain in it while you have to stop here. You are evidently not accustomed to the society of women. Therefore, as long as you are in this house, do not dare to enter this room again.

4

You see this saucepan of water on the fire? It will boil in a few seconds; it shall remain there, and I swear by the Holy Virgin, over your face I will throw it, if you as much as show your nose round the corner of that door. These gentlemen who are with you may occasionally come in if they want to—but you—git!——" and she literally brought her teeth together with a snap as she pronounced these words and pointed to the door.

"You demmed she-cat!" exclaimed Jamie, sorely amazed and taken aback.

It was a bad break. Jeannette snatched up a billet of wood from a heap alongside the stove (the Indian blood was showing now in addition to the Gallic), and in another second he would most assuredly have stopped it, in its projected career, with his head had not he ducked that turnip-like growth with a smartness that did him credit, and made a bolt for the door. Once in the little passage he found the other room, where Dick Townley and the scout at once set to work to make a good fire in the stove. It was a large, comfortable room, with a bed in a recess—indeed, it was Gabriel St. Denis' own room, and was as quaintly furnished as the kitchen. Only on a species of stand stood the mounted head of that now, alas! extinct monarch of the prairies, the great American bison. It was a truly grand specimen; there was an air of might and majesty in that picturesque, shaggy, fierce front. Jamie took a

seat moodily near the stove, and awaited an opportunity of venting his superfluous spleen on the private
or the scout.

In the meantime the sergeant had gone back into
the kitchen, and shut the door gently behind him.
He held his hat in his hands—Jamie had never
removed his—and as he stood before the two women
there was a look of unmistakable pain and humiliation upon his face. The girl had gone back to the
dresser, and had mechanically taken up her iron,
but, somehow, she did not seem as if she cared to
meet the eyes of the sergeant. And now the latter
spoke.

" I cannot tell you how ashamed and sorry I am,"
he began, apologetically, in rather an unsteady voice,
" at the annoyance you have been subjected to. The
fact of the matter is, the inspector is hardly himself
to-day, he was subjected to some slight annoyance
before we came here."

And now the girl stopped her ironing and looked
full upon the face of the dark, handsome-featured
trooper. Why should he lie for such a brute?

" Does your force produce many such specimens ? "
she inquired, with all traces of her former annoyance
gone, but with a touch of irony in her voice.

" Only one or two, thank goodness; but they do all
the mischief," was the reply. " It is not an edifying
subject to talk about such men, or how they come to
get commissions in the force. There are, however,

many officers who, if they had heard the inspector talk as he did a few minutes ago, would have knocked him down ; I am certain of that. It may be presumption on my part, but I say this for the sake of many of his brother officers whom I admire and respect as men and gentlemen. Anyhow, on behalf of my comrades of the rank and file, I should like to express my sense of shame and indignation at the insult which you were subjected to. It is very good of you to offer us even the next room to stay in, but you have only to say the word, and I can take it upon myself to promise that we shall quit it also."

"There is no occasion to do that," she said, her innate goodness of heart struggling with another motive.

She took a linen cuff from off the heap beside her, and spread it on the dresser. How beautifully rounded and symmetrical her arm was as she poised the hot iron, and how firm and delicately finished her small hand. He thought of the many fine ladies he had known in his time who would have been jealous could they but have seen such hands. He looked at that sweet, fair face, in which the light of truth shone, and he, who had in an erratic, stirring career seen all sorts and conditions of women—he who had experienced many strange phases of life, felt his heart go out to this girl with a great pity, which was only accentuated by a sense of his own helplessness to aid her.

There was a significant pause, only broken by the slight clicking noise of the iron as it travelled over the snowy cuff and the swathed board. Then old Jeannette, who knew and looked with a favourable eye upon the sergeant, being somewhat mollified by the humble and deferential tone he adopted, opened a door at the far end of the room, and went into another to perform, to her, some never-ending domestic duties.

Then the sergeant, Harry Yorke, said somewhat awkwardly—

"I have brought you these books, Miss St. Denis; I told you of them last time I was here. I was not sure that we should call upon you, but put them in my wallets in case."

Many a time had this man, when in a different station of life, given some lady of the great, gay world a much more significant token of regard without as much as the faintest suspicion of embarrassment, but now he felt like a schoolboy talking to a *débutante*, or a bashful lover who is saying his first sweet thing.

" It is very good of you to have remembered the books," she remarked, simply, but rewarding him with a pleasant look. Then that odd, apprehensive expression, which like a shadow he had seen flit across her face when they had first entered, once more crossed it. As if she had nerved herself to say something she had been pondering over, she again turned as if to face him, and, looking him steadily in the eyes, asked—

" Are you going to wait here till my father comes back ? "

He seemed ill at ease and distressed in a most unaccountable manner, this happy-go-lucky trooper. Indeed, he looked like an awkward, hulking school-boy in the presence of the head-master, who gazes with a sinister aspect upon the spectacle of conscious guilt. He tried to look away from her, but he could not. There was evidently a struggle of some sort going on within him ; of natural inclination and a sense of duty. And now these all-compelling eyes of hers seemed to have exercised their potency, for when he spoke it was as she had willed, the plain and bitter truth.

" I cannot tell you how much against my own inclination I am here on my present errand," he said, brokenly and hurriedly ; " but as I see you only desire confirmation of what you already know, it is no breach of trust on my part to admit that you are right in what you have hinted at."

He paused, as if there were something else on his mind which he did not rightly know if he would be justified in saying to her. Then he took a turn up and down the room, coming back to where she was standing calmly regarding him, with her two hands resting on the back of a chair, but still with that wistful look in her eyes that was pitiable to see.

After a brief pause he continued, somewhat coldly as she thought—

"I do not know that I should say what I am going to now, more especially as I think you have not treated me as you ought to have done. For a very long time the operations of your father have been known to the Mounted Police. For instance, they were telegraphed only a few days ago from Fort Benton to Walsh over the 'Rocky Mountain Telegraph Company's' wire. Now, Miss St. Denis, I naturally feel somewhat mortified, though I am aware you are perfectly justified in asking me by what right I express such a sentiment, when I think how I have sacrificed that fine sense of duty (which should always be paramount in a man in my position) for the sake of helping your father to free himself from the dangerous connections he has made, and how my well-meant warnings have been disregarded."

She did not tell him, as some other women might have done (either from mistaken motives of a subtle political nature peculiar to a woman's mind, or as a matter of fact), that neither she nor her father had invited this confidence on his part, or had even attempted in the very slightest degree to deceive him or dissemble when uninvited he had visited them. She only recognised the justice and truth of what he hinted at, and, pressing her hand wearily to her forehead, she waited for him to continue, which he did.

"But let us speak more plainly in order that we may not misunderstand each other. As you know, I have called several times upon your father here, just as any other civilian would, in a purely private and social capacity, and you have always been good enough to make me welcome as such. Indeed, I often have been only too glad to avail myself of the opportunity your father so kindly placed at my disposal, of spending an hour or two pleasantly that would otherwise have been spent very drearily indeed in this lonely part of the country. Of course—and I am very sorry to give you pain by referring to it again—I have always been aware of the traffic your father engaged in with Montana, and I have always, so far as I could consistently with my sense of duty, and ideas of what was proper as his guest, endeavoured to influence him against the suicidal course he is pursuing, for such a course in the end must always prove disastrous. Indeed, the very last time I was here I gave your father a very direct warning. It seems madness to me that he should have attempted another venture in the teeth of what was said on that occasion. And now we have been sent to intercept him as he comes across the lines. It will be a very serious affair for him if we get him with a contraband cargo, which he is pretty sure to have. I can assure you I dislike the painful task of arresting him only less than the necessity of having to prepare you for it."

And now the composure of the girl seemed to have deserted her. She grew very pale, and a dizziness seemed to seize her ; she swayed for a moment where she stood. The trooper caught her by the arm tenderly and respectfully, and placed her in a seat. Looking up she saw the sincerity of his great pity for her in his eyes, and it moved her strangely. But she seemed to recover as she spoke to him.

"I am afraid I am rather upset," she said, with a pitiful little smile. Then, as if unconscious of the presence of any one, she involuntarily clasped her hands in front of her, and moaned, "Oh, my poor father, it is all for me you do this thing! Goodness knows I would rather work from morning till night and live on a crust than have things as they are."

She remained for a few minutes as if buried in thought, with her hands nervously clasping each other on her lap, and her eyes looking out tearfully, and oh, so sadly, into the blurred, hurrying snowstorm. Harry Yorke stood with his hands behind his back, and a troubled expression upon his face, looking away from her into the wintry-like chaos of drifting snowflakes. Once or twice the girl stirred uneasily, and regarded the trooper intently as if she were studying him. Some struggle, some conflict of inclinations, was going on within her. Was it her maidenly pride, and that sense·of duty she owed to a parent? Her knowledge of the conventionalities of life might not have been so complete as many of her

more worldly-wise sisters in more favoured parts of
the world, but her innate maiden modesty was true
to itself and free from prudery. Modesty is always
a powerful charm in a girl when untrammelled by
false restraints. Once or twice she moved her lips as
if to speak, then checked herself. After all, on what
grounds could she claim the assistance or connivance
of this man ? He had always treated her only with
that courtly and kindly respect, which her instincts
told her was in no way different from that which he
had used towards those grand ladies of that very
different world to which he had at one time belonged.
But in the convent at Prince Albert she had mixed
with many who were ladies, both by birth and up-
bringing, and as on both her father's and her mother's
side she inherited that natural dignity and charm of
manner that has its origin in gentle blood, she, perhaps, showed a higher degree of refinement than
generally falls to girls in her sphere of life in the
Canadian North-West, so, perhaps, he could not well
treat her otherwise. Besides, she had read much,
and, what was of greater importance, she had a
natural taste for the better kind of literature of a
healthy and elevating tone, not the pessimistical,
prurient, and sickly sort that libels the present age
under the false title of the society "up-to-date"
novel. She could not presume upon any fancied
regard which he might entertain for her ; the very
idea was nauseous. Besides, in that case what would

he think of her? To throw herself upon his pity would be equally humiliating. Moreover, would it not be a direct insult to him in the honourable discharge of his duty, and be assuming a certain moral laxity in his nature, to ask him to help her in this emergency? She might just as well ask him, in as many words, to be false to his queen and country at once.

But then the thought of her father rose up before her; the days when after her mother died, and they were travelling westwards over the vast and seemingly interminable prairies with the waggons. How, many a time, to please and soothe her to sleep, he would walk for miles alongside the waggons with her in his arms. How he had helped to nurse and tend her, with all the deep-seated tenderness and devotion that his nature was capable of. How he would unbend from his seemingly austere mood, and gather flowers and play with her on the prairie for hours together, so that she might not miss the companionship of other children. How her slightest wish seemed his proud privilege to perform. How he had nursed her through long sleepless nights of illness, nor ever seemed to have but one thought or wish, and that for her. How he had parted with her, when she had gone to the convent on the Saskatchewan, in what she knew was a spirit of self-sacrifice, in order that she might not grow up as ignorant as many of the children in that great lone land. Even now, if her

father had broken the laws of the country, something
told her it was no mere greed of gain on his part—
personally he was the most unselfish of men—that
had led him to do this, but that he eventually might
be able to bring her into a sphere of life which would
be more congenial than the present one. "Oh, father,
father!" she repeated to herself, as the image of his
kindly, time-worn face rose up before her, from that
wonderful magic-mirror of the mind, and which she
knew and loved so well. One course lay open to her,
and she did not hesitate to contemplate it : where
only the matter of her own personal safety and
physical well-being were concerned. Her eyes were
undimmed now ; rising she went towards the window
and looked out.

"Do you think we shall have much of a blizzard ?"
she inquired.

"It is impossible to say, but I hope not," he
answered.

Then, as if it were in answer to some project she
had just communicated to him, he continued—

"But you must not think of going out in such a
storm ; you would lose your way before you went
sixty yards. Besides, if the inspector thought you
meditated any such thing he would not scruple to
put you under some embarrassing restraints."

"Does that man control my movements?" she
asked, somewhat indignantly. "The day is past
when the North-West Mounted Police relegated to

themselves rights that even the Russian Police would hardly dare to take."

"No," he answered, humbly, coming towards the window and standing opposite her; "but you must recollect that he is not a——"

"Yes, I understand, and will spare you the pain of the admission."

"Thanks. I wish I could help you," he continued, "but you can understand my position. I am not blameless in my own eyes now, telling you what I have done."

Still he kept his eyes averted from hers, and tried to concentrate his gaze upon the hurrying snow-flakes; but that was a difficult thing to do.

And now the girl nerved herself for her self-imposed task. As if to fix his attention she placed one hand lightly upon his arm, and he was forced to look at her. Somehow, to him, this seemed a natural and simple action coming from her. He knew it was a dangerous and fatal thing for him to look at her; but then he was in no way different from other men, although he belonged to a calling that is supposed to eliminate from its exercise anything approaching sentiment. She was a very beautiful girl indeed; but whether it was a sense of pity for her, or the witchery of her superior presence that influenced him, he did not speculate upon just then.

"You will perhaps forget what I am going to say now," she said, catching her breath quickly, "if it

appears to you an unfair and unwomanly thing of me
to ask. Of course, I have no claim on your consideration whatever, but I somehow think you would
rather help me than otherwise. I am not going to
insult you by asking you to avoid your duty; but I
should like you to bear in mind my position. You
must know my father is everything in this life to me,
and I would not think twice of risking my life in the
chance of saving his; though I know he would
consider such a sacrifice wasted were I to lose mine.
Perhaps you can understand this."

He did not speak, but simply bowed his head.

She went on again—

"I know that wherever he is on the prairie at
present, he is safe enough—he has weathered too
many blizzards. As long as this one lasts he is safe
enough from you; but, of course, you know he may
pull in here any time it lifts. What I want to ask of
you is that you promise me not to interfere with my
movements whenever the snow may stop. It may be
nothing to you that I promise my father shall never
offend again ; but it shall be so. It may not be such
a very great thing to ask of you after all, but it means
everything to me. Perhaps I might be more certain
of the success of my plans were I to keep my own
counsel; but I have reasons for this step, and would
rather feel that you were with me. Will you do as
I want you to?"

Her hand still rested lightly, and as if unconsciously,

upon his wrist; and her touch seemed to thrill him as no touch had ever done before. At the close of her appeal she had withdrawn her eyes from his face, as if she were conscious of having said more than prudence dictated. With that great gleaming wealth of silky hair surrounding her beautiful face like an aureole : watching the downward glance of these delicately veined eyelids, and with that mobile face so near to his, he would have been more than human could he have done otherwise than he did. She had thrown herself as it were upon his mercy. She had shown that she had faith in his natural goodness of heart. And, after all, it was not for herself she pleaded, but for a father. She had not asked him to do anything that was in any way disgraceful, she had merely asked him, what it was unnecessary for her to have asked, not to interfere with her movements when the storm had lifted. Besides, doubtless knowing that the inspector was brute enough to lock two defenceless women up, if he suspected that they might spoil his contemplated seizure, she reckoned that he, the sergeant, having her confidence, might possibly dissuade him from any such arbitrary measures. But was it necessary to ask his assistance at all? She might have known that with the exception of the inspector himself, none of the others would have dreamt of interfering with her movements. No, not even, perhaps, if they had suspected her designs. Could it be that on account of their slight intimacy in the past, she did not wish to appear as if stealing a march on him? Some people had such a fine sense of honour as to the relations between one person and another, even although these relations hinged on a matter of dubious principle. This thought, somehow, thrilled him with a certain secret satisfaction.

Their eyes met for a second, but neither spoke. Then, by an impulse that he could hardly account for, the trooper performed a good old-fashioned, chivalric action that has, somehow, gone out of fashion in these more prosaic modern times. He caught up one of her hands, and bowing his head over it, lightly pressed it to his lips; and she knew that he had granted her request.

And then he left the room abruptly.

CHAPTER V.

HER MANY MOODS.

WHEN Marie was left alone, she stood for a long time gazing out upon the blurred and dreary prospect that the external world presented. But, perhaps, she never saw it, for her eyes had that far-away look that denotes the mind to be engaged in other than its immediate surroundings. When the trooper had kissed her hand she had not attempted, nor indeed did she desire, to withdraw it. She was no prude, and she interpreted that old-time action as any other sensible girl would have interpreted it. Perhaps, however, it might have sent an extra tinge of colour into her cheek, and a shyer and gladder light might have dawned in her eyes. As has been said, they were beautiful eyes at any time; but there was a light in them now that had not been in them before. Her spirits gradually rose as a certain definite plan revealed itself to her. She felt as if she must occupy herself with something or other, or else her hectic spirits would break through all

5

restraints and lead her into some foolishness. She looked at the books which the trooper had placed upon the dresser for her. "And I never even said 'thank you' to him," she said, fearfully, and with a dawning sense of recollection. Then Jeannette came back into the room, and away her quick thoughts flew on a new tack.

"Oh, Jeannette! By the way," she said, "I wonder if the police have got their own food with them?"

"Sure, sure, honey. They always carry everything about with them. An old police hand can almost cook a meal in the face of a blizzard. But even if they have not, do you think they hev' any call on you; 'specially that pig-like man with the little gilt crown on the collar of his pretty little red coat. Ouf! the beast!" And old Jeannette vigorously shoved a billet of wood into the small cooking stove, as if it were the inspector she were placing there for crema- tion. The old lady's very decided animus evidently amused Marie, who continued—

"But, Jeannette, the others are not like him; for instance, that nice little fat man, Pierre, with the black, beady, twinkling eyes, although, perhaps, his waist is not quite so slim as one could wish it to be. And there is that young policeman—such a dear, curly-headed little fellow. I declare I've almost a mind to fall in love with him; or I wonder if I could get him to fall in love with me? And then the sergeant——" here she stopped abruptly, and did not say anything more about him. But she laughed almost gaily as she continued—"Then, Jeannette, let us make some pancakes—we've lots of maple-syrup ·—and send them into the next room. You know it might possibly put that dreadful thing, whom you call the "houkimo," into a somewhat better humour. I am sure that through the stomach is one way of reaching that sort of creature, anyhow." And Marie rattled on as if under the influence of a strong reaction of spirits.

"By the blessed Virgin, and what may be the matter with my honey?" cried the keen-eyed Jeannette, regarding Marie wonderingly.

She had never seen the girl in such spirits before. She had expected since the arrival of the police that the girl would suddenly break down, and that she— Jeannette—would have to comfort her, and have to advance all sorts of fictitious hopes regarding her father's ultimate safety. But here she was labouring under an almost hectic flow of spirits, and even proposing to entertain those who were about to bring disgrace and misery upon her and hers. *Ma fois!* It was a strange world. Jeannette, for all the years she had lived in it, could hardly understand it. Jeannette belonged to that lower order of beings with whom the luxury of nerves and their vagaries is supposed to be an unknown quantity. She remembered how in Old Fort Garry, in the gay old days before the Wolseley Expedition, when two or three of the head officials in the Hudson Bay Company's service had brought up their wives with them, she had taken service with one of them. These gay creatures of *le beau monde* came from Montreal or Quebec, and had in their time even visited these almost mythical over-sea cities, London and Paris. Therefore, their manners and little ways to the sturdy and simple children of the great North-West passed all understanding. She could remember how, occasionally—as if to vary the monotony of their lives—whenever they happened to have differences of opinion with their lords and masters, or after labouring under any unusual mental excitement, they inevitably resorted to one potent and unanswerable argument—hysterics. Could Marie's unwonted conduct be another form of this recondite disease? Jeannette knew that this girl's mother belonged to that superior order of beings, with whom the possession of delicately strung nerves is an hereditary attribute. This she knew just as truly as that the girl's capacity for suiting herself naturally to such company as chance threw in her way, and still showing that she was superior to it, was another.

Jeannette, therefore, in order to counteract any further development of the symptoms already referred to, hastened to humour her young mistress, and getting out the flour, &c., prepared to make the pancakes, which, by the way, is a popular dish on the American continent. She, however, resolved to keep an eye on her young mistress, and determined if that "pig-like brute of an officer," put as much as a foot over the threshold of the kitchen to annoy her young mistress, to find out whether his head or a billet of wood were the harder. Upon this point Jeannette had her doubts.

As the old lady indulged in these speculations there was a knock at the door. It opened, and a buffalo-coated figure appeared in the doorway. Now, the law of association is a powerful thing, and Jeannette's hand darted like a flash of lightning to the rolling-pin, and her lips framed that significant word, " git ! " In another second, Dick Townley, the private, would have met with an impressive reception had not he darted back in alarm.

" Hold hard there, madam ! " he cried in alarm. " It's not Pudding-head—I mean the inspector." " The devil ! " he said to himself, " what an old fire-brand it is to be sure."

" Oh, it is you, is it ? *Entrer,*" cried old Jeannette, with an apologetic smile upon her face. " Why did not you say who you were at first ? It would have been a matter of regret with me if I had caused the death of one so young."

The youth looked sheepishly upon the face of Marie, who was sitting with her head slightly thrown back and evidently much amused. Indeed, it would have been a difficult matter for any one to have refrained from laughing at the sight of the young

trooper's evident alarm, on his catching a glimpse
of that uplifted arm and rolling-pin.

"Indeed, madam," said the polite and talkative
youth in answer to Jeannette, " I was not aware that
your personal animus to my superior officer was to
take such a practical and forcible expression." He
paused, shut the door behind him carefully as if to
prevent the sound of their voices from reaching the
other room, and, with an expressive grin upon his
face, continued in a somewhat lower voice, "And I
hope you will let him have it good and hard when
you do give it him. I can assure you, it's the only
way that any expression of an absence of sympathy
with his style will ever be brought home to him."

He paused again, then said, as if it had only
suggested itself to him. " But if you've got any oak
or pine, use that—cotton-wood is too soft, and would
make no impression. You see, it's difficult to believe
how thick that man's skull is."

And now he seemed somewhat diffident, and his
eyes wandered round the room. Then, as if he had
found what he wanted, he caught up the two empty
buckets and hurried out again.

"Good boy; gone to fetch some water," explained
Jeannette.

"What a nice face; and what a beautiful curly head
of hair he has," said the girl, abstractedly. She was
in a dangerous mood now; for it is a remarkable
psychological paradox, that it is often the most un-

likely and the soberest individuals who, on occasions,
do and say the maddest and most incomprehensible
things. " But he seems rather self-conscious," she
continued, " and as if he were almost afraid of a girl.
I wonder if he has ever kissed one. Jeannette, you
wont look, will you, if I kiss him ? "

" *Pardonnez moi, Jeannette. Do, like a good soul,
go into the next room for only half a minute, and just
give her a chance.*"

And to the horror and confusion of poor Marie,
the youthful trooper—who had been in the passage
all the time pulling on his mitts—again put his
head into the room, and smiled in a fashion that
was hardly in accordance with the diffidence with
which he was accredited. Marie fairly put her hands
up to hide her face, which, judging from the colour
that had mounted into her beautiful throat and neck,
must have been of a tell-tale crimson. She had never
before in her life made such a bold speech ; and it
seemed, to her innocent mind, as if it were a special
dispensation of Providence that she should be caught
in the very act of making it, and covered with confusion.

As for Jeannette her suspicions were confirmed.
Her dear and modest young mistress had contracted
that mysterious disease which she had seen, in another
form, compel high-born dames to throw about china
ornaments, to use absurd and incomprehensible language, and generally misconduct themselves. To

think that this poor girl, whom she had hardly ever
before heard mention the name of a man, should
actually talk about forcibly kissing one, was something that almost took away her breath. Or, could
it be that her knowledge of the double risk and
danger her father ran just then had temporarily
unhinged her reason ? She—Jeannette—would look
up that bag of Indian medicinal roots and herbs,
which she resorted to in cases of emergency, and
would probably find some potent medicine, which
would counteract and arrest the progress of the
disease, for such she regarded it.

So far as the youthful member of the police force
himself was concerned, who had been the innocent
cause of all the trouble, he was the least concerned
of the three. It would have rather surprised the two
women and added to their peace of mind, could
they have known that this not-so-bashful-as-he
appeared-to-be young man, was in no way shocked
by the unblushing declaration of poor Marie. For
had he not in his time been in the company of jolly,
light-hearted, and, perhaps, not a little mischievously
inclined English girls, who had not only threatened
to kiss him (not under the mistletoe either), but had
actually done it too. And he had not thought much
about it either ; for he had been one of those enviable
ones who, for certain reasons being made much of,
grow accustomed to attentions that would turn the
heads of less favoured individuals, and who even

come to look upon such attentions as theirs by natural right. Therefore, the diffidence of this ingenuous youth was indeed a refreshing thing, and often surprised the unsophisticated. But his halcyon days in the old country had been all too brief; for, like many more younger sons of younger sons, he had been packed off to Manitoba to learning farming. There finding the task of expostulating with perverse oxen, and milking deceitful cows, hardly the idyllic and congenial employment he had imagined it to be, he had, like many more of his kind, drifted into the ranks of the North-West Mounted Police, there to moralise with kindred spirits over "joys departed never to return."

And now, as he went to the covered well, he bowed his head to the icy blast. "By Jove," he said to himself, " who would have dreamt of seeing a girl like that in this God-forsaken part of the world? But she's only like all the rest of them. The girl who looks as if she were thinking of heaven all the time, and who you think only requires a pair of wings to make her an angel, is, probably, thinking of nothing higher than man's gullibility, and wondering if the right chap will have sand enough to come forward at the right time. But I'll have that kiss yet in spite of the old lady."

But he did not have that kiss.

CHAPTER VI.

THE blizzard raged for a couple of days. The snow then ceased falling, but the fierce wind hurried the dry, powdery, crystalline flakes along over the exposed and far-stretching prairie in one dense and cloud-like sheet, making it impossible for any one to see five yards ahead. And still it was a paradoxical thing, when one came to think of it, that the sun shone brilliantly down all the time, and lit up that ghostly but tangible atmosphere of snow, till it became instinct with rings of prismatic colouring, and spark-led as if it were a shower of fine diamonds. This is, perhaps, the one great redeeming feature in this great lone land in the long winter-time. What, indeed, may be said to give it a life peculiarly its own : for were there no shading in Nature's pictures, then would the comparative effects of light and colour be meaning-less. No matter how the blizzard rages, no matter how the quicksilver sinks in the thermometer—30°, 40°, 50° below zero—and over the silent and illimitable stretches of snow-clad, wind-swept prairie Jack Frost securely reigns, the all-enlivening and encircling sun generally shines down uninterruptedly from a cloud-less sky through it all. Ghastly and desolate indeed would be that ocean-like surface of rolling prairie without its cheering rays : a shipless sea in a region of eternal twilight would not be more weirdly melancholy.

In Gabriel St. Denis' room the officer, the sergeant, the private, and the scout passed the time as they best could. The officer and the scout had, doubtless, the best of the situation. The first mentioned was so happily constituted by nature that he never felt the leaden wings of Time. He could, like a thought-reader, when he wishes to receive an impression or a brain-wave, allow his mind to become a perfect blank, in which he existed in an almost trance-like state. Generally speaking, this was Jamie's normal condition ; only it needed no great exercise of will power on his part to arrive at this happy state : there were seldom any thoughts to get rid of in his brain. And as for receiving impressions—unless they were unpleasant ones—it would have required more than the hypo-thetical surgical operation associated with Scotsmen to inoculate him with one. It would have required some violent shock to the system—something of the nature of wood or iron brought in forcible contact with his bullet-like head—to arouse in him the faintest suspicion of intellectual activity. He would

lie on his back, stretched on a buffalo-robe in front of
the stove, for hours at a stretch, and gaze vacantly at
the ceiling. The only part of the day in which he
seemed to evince any interest was meal-time.

On the day of their coming the scout had been
summoned to the kitchen by Jeannette shortly after
mid-day, and coming back he had spread the table
with a snow-white cloth, and brought in, much to
Jamie's surprise and delight, a dish of hot potatoes,
some cold venison, a dish of steaming and juicy bear-
steaks, and a large dish of pancakes with maple syrup.
On this occasion Jamie showed signs of returning
consciousness such as he had never before been seen
to exhibit. Moreover, he was heard to exclaim as
he rubbed his hands together, "Well, I'm darned!"
After this mental feat, and for the next twenty
minutes, his mouth was too full to permit of his
entertaining the company with any further exhibi-
tions of his conversational powers. They all sat down
at the same table together ; for on the prairie this
is the usual way. The meal passed in comparative
silence ; the sergeant seemed to be engrossed with
his own thoughts, the officer's—if he had any—were
concentrated upon the bear-steaks, and the youthful
trooper and the scout soon allowed the light and
cheerful tone of banter, in which they had at first
indulged, to gradually subside. For the sight of their
officer's face had a depressing effect. At last the
latter could eat no more, and rising from the table

left the room to have a look at the horses in the stable.

A stable was to Jamie what a drawing-room would have been to one of his more civilised brother officers. He felt, literally, at home in the stable : the absence of conventionality there, and something in its very odour suggested congenial environment. He was in the habit of spending many hours, when he could manage it, with a straw in his mouth surveying the equine race. He felt perfectly at ease in the company of horses.

On the occasion referred to, when he had left the room, Dick Townley, the private, laid down his knife and fork, and for a few moments indulged in a quiet laugh. The sergeant asked him what was amusing him.

" I wonder, when he's in the mess-room at Regina," said the youth, referring to his departed superior, " if he eats with his knife as he does here, dips his fingers into the salt-cellars, and, otherwise, does so many extraordinary things ? But I have forgotten—he is a married man, so don't suppose he will often honour the mess with his presence."

" You bet your boots," chimed in the little scout, who prided himself upon his superior manners ; " when I down in Regina was once, the waiter in the officer's mess did in confidence communicate to me that on one occasion when Monsieur was dining in the mess—the Commissioner and a number of guests were there—he spilt his *potage* all over the table, used his fingers *à la fourchette*, and when those—finger glasses I believe it is you will call them—were brought in, he did stare upon them, and asked if there was going to be a christening match. *Mon Dieu*—these are pancakes *magnifique*."

"Oh, come now, you fellows," said the sergeant who, however, could not conceal a smile ; "your talk is of a highly treasonable nature. Why can't you leave your superior officer alone ? By the way, we must not allow those women to send in food like this to us. It makes me feel horribly ashamed when I think of their kindness, considering our errand here ; but, as the boss won't think of thanking them, I shall go in and do so myself later on. I wonder if we could annex a cross-cut saw somewhere ; I don't believe in burning other people's fire-wood for nothing ; but I noticed an out-house at the back, perhaps we could get a few logs into it, and cut up sufficient wood for the whole lot of us. In the meantime, I'm going out to look after their cattle in the corral. I wonder if they have any water in their buckets in the next room ; you might just go in and see, Pierre. I wonder which of the women made these pancakes—they are superb ? "

Here Dick Townley said—without looking up, however, "You needn't bother, Pierre. I filled their buckets some little time ago."

"Indeed ! that was thoughtful of you," said the

sergeant, somewhat surprised, and with an impenetrable smile.

"Why, what are you grinning at, Yorke?" pursued the irreverent youngster, with not a little annoyance showing in his voice. "Can't a fellow carry a bucket or two of water for a woman, without you seeing something funny in it?"

"Oh, certainly, certainly; keep your coat on, my boy," was the answer, still with that odd smile. "I might have known that some one would be gallant enough to render a service in that direction. But you haven't told me what you think of Mademoiselle St. Denis yet, Dick. Don't you think a girl is bound to vegetate in such a place?"

Now, Dick Townley had no particular desire to discuss the merits of this girl with his comrade : he had, somehow, not thought the latter had sufficient interest in the fair sex to converse intelligibly on such a momentous subject. His first impression, when he had seen Marie St. Denis, had been one of surprise and admiration at discovering such a *rara avis* in such an unlikely place. Certainly he had heard rumours regarding her good looks; but had ascribed them to the usual delusive talk peculiar to Mounted Policemen, who, in their isolated position by a law of Nature, take every bird to be a jay, and the plainest-featured women the personification of female loveliness. Moreover, after the, to him, flattering speech he had overheard the girl give utterance

to, he had resolved to cultivate her acquaintance.
Being only human, and not wanting in worldly
wisdom, he had refrained from openly expressing his
admiration of her, in case his superior might take
it into his head to step in before him and spoil a
projected and agreeable flirtation. It was, therefore,
with not a little surprise he heard his usually reticent
comrade ask him for his opinion of the girl. The
ingenuous youth felt flattered, and replied with an air
of superior knowledge of the subject in question.

"Well, Yorke," he said, "since you've asked me
for my opinion I'll give it you. I believe that girl's
a brick, a regular little brick, and as good as she's
good-looking. I don't mean to say either that she's
one of your milk-and-water sort ; because, I believe,
she's just as fond of a lark as any other girl. But
where and how she has picked up her manners and
style gets over me—why, she would pass muster as a
lady any day. I would not be surprised if there was
a drop of good blood in her. She talks beautifully,
and from her hands and feet to her teeth and eyes
there is not one faulty point about her. So far as
dress goes, though she is simplicity itself, in those
dainty little white collars and cuffs of hers there are
infinite possibilities. To use a rather hackneyed
phrase she is 'a prairie rose.' 'But the flowers that
bloom in the Spring tra-la, have nothing to do with
the case.'" And as if to divert attention from his
rather eulogistic and somewhat rambling opinion,

he broke out into a well-known Gilbertian rhyme.

The sergeant looked out of the window for a minute, and smiled grimly. Then, as if impelled to say something, he said in a tone that was meant to convey an impression of half-heartedness in the subject, but was of a peculiar dryness and significance—

"And so she is a regular little brick is she? and she is fond of a lark? In fact, as our superior officer would characteristically put it, she has several good points in her general get-up. By Jove, Dick, she would feel flattered, I'm sure, if she could only hear your estimate of her. As for there being a strain of good 'blood' in her as you remark—why, hang it, man "—and he turned suddenly from the window and faced the somewhat surprised youth—" talking about blood, did some of the names that even these half-breeds have in this country never strike you? Don't you know that, generally speaking, and in comparison with their numbers, there are more representatives of a noble and historical aristocracy in Canada than there are in France? though some of them are humble and poor enough now, goodness only knows. Now, just listen to a few of the names you meet with in this country—names that people have grown so familiar with, that no one attaches any significance to them: St. Denis, St. Cloud, St. Arnaud, La Fontaine, L'Esperance, St. Croix, Xavier, and many others.

6

Why, the forefathers of some of those people our parvenus hardly know were noblemen long before William the Conqueror took a trip over to Anglia. As to who her mother was I neither know nor care. Jeannette, however, says she came of good stock. But while we are on this subject, don't misunderstand me; if the girl's name were Smith or Robinson she might still be every whit as much of a lady as she is now—the 'rank is but the guinea stamp,' after all, and is too often put on deuced inferior metal. But, since you are on this racket, I may say she bears a name that is as good, if not better, than most borne by our English aristocracy: and you advance the speculation that she has a drop of good blood !"

He stopped abruptly and laughed in a silent and significant fashion. Then he continued, as if arguing the matter out with himself—

" No ; the race that took a score of generations to develope hereditive traits and patrician graces cannot have altered so much in two or three generations, even although the lot of the latter has been a hand-to-hand struggle with adverse circumstances in a strange, new country, and with stern surroundings."

Then, as if conscious that he had betrayed a little more interest and warmth in his treatment of the subject than there was any occasion for, he added, with rather a feeble laugh—

" But all this is unimportant, and I don't care a rap

for one woman more than for another. But at the
same time, I can't help thinking it is a confounded
shame of old St. Denis to tempt Providence, and
bring disgrace upon the girl as he is doing, knowing
that she is breaking her heart over it all the time.
There is nothing of the money grub about her that
there is about the father; she is good-hearted, sensitive and proud, and, by Jove, she has got the right
metal in her, too! I never saw Jamie get such a
complete taking down before, not even when the
late Assistant Commissioner snubbed him in the
Orderly Room for trying to bully a corporal."

And here he broke off in what, for him, was an
unusually long speech, and lit his pipe. He was
unpleasantly conscious of the fact that his talk was
becoming of a rather wild and personal nature. He
was also aware of the fact, that by saying he did not
care for one woman more than for another, he spoke
as if he had been charged with so doing, when, indeed,
nobody had dreamt of hinting at such a thing. But
now the ill-concealed look of surprise and significant
silence of his comrade brought it home to him that
he had betrayed an interest in Marie St. Denis which
he wished to avoid expressing, far less feel.

But there is no royal immunity granted from the
promptings of the human heart. Artificial surroundings and conventionalities may shield us from many
wayward longings; but give the princess an opportunity of recognising an affinity in the person of the

plebeian ; then, all the laws and philosophy of Man
that ever have been, or may be, brought to bear in
assisting to destroy the attachment so mysteriously
formed, cannot and never shall remove that unseen
but potent bond that knits together two kindred
souls. But there was no one going to interfere between Harry Yorke and any one whom he should
chance to feel attracted by, unless, indeed, the im-
pediments were of his own making. But he made a
common mistake in supposing that his own particular
past, and its experiences, would make him proot
against all emotional promptings in the future. His
had been a natural enough, if not a common experience. He had been brought up to better things
than his station in life would now have indicated.
He had enjoyed his brief but bright existence, as a
man of fashion and pleasure, while it had lasted.
But evil days, which come to most of us, came to
him, and the only thing that would have saved him
from ruin—marriage with a rich but proud girl—he
had not the courage to essay. He told himself, and
truly, that had he remained in his former independent
position he would undoubtedly have asked her to
marry him, even although she could show a sovereign
for every shilling he could. But what other con-
struction could the world possibly put on his conduct
if he asked her to marry him, now that he was
penniless, than that it was purely sordid and
mercenary ? And what would the girl herself think ?

Perhaps, about this time, he began to regret that he
had let so many golden opportunities slip ; for he
had really admired her. But it was too late : his
pride was too strong for him, and he had left England
without as much as saying good-bye. In six months
time he heard that the heiress was married, and
inconsistently he jeered at woman's inconsistency.
Perhaps he did not know that the woman, whom in
particular he jeered at, had hailed at first with almost
satisfaction the news of his ruined prospects ; for she
had thought the gay world would not have the same
hold on him, and she might win a fuller share of his
affections—indeed, she had been ready and waiting
to accept him if he only brought a moiety of that
desired love for her, and nothing else. She would
win it all in time. But, perhaps, she had not
understood him. She gave him every encouragement
and sign of her preference consistent with a woman's
modesty and self-respect. But his overweening pride
had blinded him, and he could not see things in
their proper light. In an impulsive spirit, born of
mortification and pique, she had married. For some
years, doubtless, his attitude towards women had been
of a reprehensible and cynical nature. But, latterly,
a more rational spirit had come to him, and he had
seen clearly enough that he, and not the woman, had
been in the wrong. But the experience had influenced
him ; perhaps, not for the better in a worldly point of
view, for it had deadened ambition in him, and caused

him to pass through life as if his highest object
in it were merely the acquiring of strange and novel
experiences. He thought he had done with the one
great experience of life. He was not aware of the
fact that he had deluded himself, and that he had
not really loved : for if he had, he would either have
married the heiress and snapped his fingers at what
the world might think, or else he would not have
tamely submitted to a supposititious Inevitable, without making some endeavour to overcome it.

Doubtless, the dawning of the truth upon him by the
awakening of a feeling that he had not dreamt himself
capable of, brought home the accusation to him, that
in his concentration on self he had caused others to
suffer. The natural laws of retributive justice may
be slow, but they are sure. In the dawn of a new
life that he struggled against, he was haunted by the
upbraiding shadows of an old one.

CHAPTER VII.

AN UNCONSCIOUS PRECEPTOR.

A COUPLE of days had passed, the snow-laden winds still blew fiercely, and the police party were kept close prisoners in St. Denis' ranche. As for the inspector, he continued to enjoy long spells of mental abstraction, lying on his buffalo-robe on the floor before the stove, with his eyes fixed upon the ceiling. At long intervals, when he recognised the necessity of varying this species of entertainment, he would adjourn to the stable, where, sticking a straw in his mouth, he would keep the horses company for half an hour at a stretch. It was a redeeming point in his character that he seemed fond of animals. "A fellow feeling makes us wondrous kind." Surely Nature made a mistake when she gave Jamie some semblance of a man ; had she, for instance, made him a donkey—a four-legged one, of course—he might have posed as her supreme masterpiece.

As for the sergeant, he seemed strangely ill at ease. He could not settle to read. The friendly little

wordy spars between his youthful comrade and the
cheery little scout seemed to have lost all attraction
for him ; and as for indulging in conversation with
his superior officer, as they had not two ideas in
common, that was not to be thought of. The mere
fact of the officer being comparatively uneducated
would not have mattered in itself, but Jamie, having
by contact with his brother officers become aware of
his deficiencies, dreaded to expose his ignorance
more than he could help. Moreover, being of a jealous nature, he imagined that when an educated man
talked to him it was simply for the purpose of mysti-
fying and ridiculing him. His normal condition
therefore, when with his intellectual superiors, was
like a bear with a sore head. Jamie, however, would
probably have liked to go into the other room, and
see a little more of that interesting girl whom he
had honoured so openly by expressions of his admiration. But having heard the cunning little scout
whisper to the private (as if he feared being overheard), that the dipper still remained full of boiling
water upon the stove in the next room, he lost all
interest in the girl, and came to the conclusion that
to talk to one in her position was derogatory to the
dignity of an officer of the North-West Mounted
Police force.

The others had sawn and cut up sufficient firewood
to last the little household for a month, and stacked
it neatly in one of the out-houses. They had kept

the buckets full of water, thrown down some hay for the few head of cattle in the corral, and done other necessary work about the place. Indeed, in pure gallantry, Dick Townley in spite of the protestations and warnings of Marie St. Denis (whom he seemed very anxious to favour with his attentions), would insist on one occasion on milking a certain cow, which the girl warned him though quiet enough generally, would probably resent the ministrations of a stranger. But the polite youth scouted the idea, and taking the pail from her hand started in to milk. When he picked himself up a few seconds later in a dirty and dazed condition from the neighbourhood of the opposite wall, and wondered where his cap and the pail had got to, he wisely concluded that it was a mistake, and beneath the dignity of a Mounted Policeman to associate himself in any shape or form with such an ungrateful and stupid animal as a cow.

The sergeant on the afternoon of the second day, as if he could endure his own company no longer, had left his comrades amusing themselves according to their several ideas, and betook himself to the next room. Marie St. Denis looked up from the book she was reading, and there was a quick and pleased re-cognition on her face as she saw who the visitor was ; so perhaps, after all, there was no necessity for ex-pressing it in words. Old Jeannette motioned him a chair near the stove, and told him to sit down. The thoughtful and helpful ways of the troopers had

commended themselves to her ; and, moreover, when
she considered that they were under the absolute
authority of her pet antipathy, the inspector, her
sympathetic nature regarded them with a great pity.

"I see you have still got the inspector's shaving water
on the stove, Jeannette," said the sergeant, cheerily.

" Sure, sure," said the old lady, " and the skunk will
have it yet if he puts as much as his nose inside the
door."

The girl had laid aside her book and was looking
into the stove. Her two hands were folded on her
lap in front of her ; through the mica slats in the
stove the ruddy firelight gleamed and flickered upon
her characteristically beautiful face and figure : she
made a pretty picture. Then she gazed abstractedly
at the glimmering of some of old Jeannette's burnished culinary appliances as they hung against the
opposite wall ; but she seemed diffident in regard to
looking at her visitor. He, again, scrutinised her
thoughtfully for a few minutes without speaking.
He noted the erect and beautiful poise of her head
upon these graceful shoulders, the smallness and
faultless symmetry of her hands and feet, her clearly
cut and expressive features, that faint suspicion of
the sun's kiss on her soft cheek, and the simple
perfection of her plain, dark, close-fitting dress, only
relieved by the dainty white cuffs and collar. Hers
was not merely a physically beautiful face, but it was
an intellectually beautiful one ; and not mere cold

intellectuality—for intellect, in itself, is a cold thing—
but there was in it that indefinable something that
defies analysis—that which men try to express when
they use the word "soul."

"What have you been reading?" he asked her at
length.

"An Australian story," she answered; "perhaps
hardly a woman's book, but it is an exciting one, and
I have been reading it to Jeannette, who likes it
immensely. There is an awful abyss in it called
'Terrible Hollow,' where the bushrangers used to
hide; it is the sort of place to haunt one's imagination. Now, you have been in Australia; if I recollect rightly you told us so once. Do you think there
ever was such a place as that hollow?" and she
looked at him inquiringly.

"I think there are many such places," he said
simply, "and one in particular, called the Grose
Valley, in the Blue Mountains of New South Wales,
that the author took his description from when he
pictured Terrible Hollow. Indeed, I spent several
days in it myself in '83."

"Oh, do tell us about it," cried the girl, her eyes lighting up with expectation. "This is positively interesting. Jeannette, didn't I tell you there was such a place,
and that if any one could tell us anything about it,
it was Mr. Yorke! Now, just imagine that Jeannette
and I are a couple of big children, and that we are
dying to know all about this place. Begin."

Perhaps it was the one thing that this usually reticent man most loved to talk about—the great works and wonders of Nature that he had met with in the course of his nomadic career. And now he told them, in a simple, modest way, that had no suspicion of pedantry about it, concerning this wild, almost subterraneous valley. As he warmed to his task he lost sight of his surroundings, and described it with characteristic, graphic touches that held his listeners as if spellbound. They could almost believe they were in that far off Austral land. He pictured to them that great jagged rent on the table-land of the Blue Mountains, that seemed to pierce into the very bowels of the earth, and whose sides went down sheer and precipitously for four thousand feet at a bound. How, viewed from the verge of this yawning, nightmarish abyss, the white-limbed giant eucalypti, immense tree ferns, and monstrous fantastic old-world flora, lurking in places where the sun never shone, were hardly discernible to the naked eye ; and where, indeed, the pitiless, adamantine walls of rock made a twilight even in the daytime. And how that cold and crystal stream that hurried through it, flung in the first place from the dizzy heights of Govett's leap, pierced its way between cyclopean blocks of sandstone, and through black subterranean passages—a veritable river of Styx—until it emerged into the bright sunshine again, on the other and lower side of the mountain, to form the

Nepean river and help to swell the lordly Hawkesbury. Of such a place Milton or Dante might have dreamed.

But suddenly recollecting himself he stopped short. Though he had the powers of a born narrator he had no inordinate opinion of himself; now he asked himself, in a spirit of irony, if he were graduating for the lecture platform.

"Why did you not stop me?" he cried, almost resentfully, "how I must have bored you? When I get wound up on such subjects there is no holding me; like the Saskatchewan, I go on for ever."

But the girl did not seem even to notice this self-depreciating speech. As she had listened to his description the interest upon her face had become intense; she had sat in a state of rapt attention, her hands clasped before her resting on her knees. Then slowly she seemed to awake from wandering in that quaint old-world valley—the deepest valley with perpendicular cliffs in the known world—to the stern snow-bound world of the frozen North, and the change was a remarkable one, truly. As for Jeannette, she had sat with wide-open eyes and tingling ears, as if she listened to some of La Salle's adventures in the days of *le bois coureurs.* Australia seemed a farther off and more mythical country to her than that happy hunting ground of the Ojibiways and the Crees. She felt a wholesome respect for a man who could tell of such wonderful places, and at the same time hardly talk of himself at all.

"Now," said the girl, "this book has an interest for me that it had not before. But it is a sad book, and the moral is so evident——"

She checked herself abruptly as if she had said more than she intended to say.

"Yes," he said, musingly, and with an unconscious, pitiless candour, "apart from the moral conveyed, it is simply the history of a natural sequence obeying one of Nature's just laws. It is the inevitable tragedy which waits upon those lives whose downward career has begun by some apparently trifling divergency from the obvious path of duty, until passion or the sordid love of gain has perverted the moral eyesight, and death alone can break the spell that binds the infatuated victim. Just think of those misguided men being shot down like wild animals by the troopers——"

He in his turn stopped abruptly. What on earth was he talking about to this girl? He had entirely lost sight of the awkward parallel and personal bearing that the imaginary case he had been discussing had upon the surroundings of this girl's own life. Had he forgotten what he was, and what he was there for? Was it not bad enough to have unthinkingly put into this innocent girl's hands a book having such a direct personal application without parading his views upon it, and running the risk of being considered as playing the part of a moral preceptor, though, to do him justice, nothing had been further from his thoughts. He fairly bit his lips with vexation at the false light he must appear in to this girl.

And now, how could he right himself in her eyes without making matters worse? It was such a delicate subject, and must surely only bring further pain and humiliation upon her. Surely she could not deem him guilty of such candid brutality. Fearfully he stole a look at her.

And she, with that subtle intuition which some women possess, saw that he had suddenly realised what misconstruction might be put upon his unguarded moralising. She was also true enough to her womanly nature to feel not a little secret gratification in the fact that the thought of it distressed him. Had it not, then, it would have indicated lack of interest in her. She saw the horns of the dilemma he was on, and it was a touch of the spirit of old Mother Eve that made her affect to believe him guilty.

"Oh, of course, you are right," she said, coldly, after a pause, "and I ought to feel obliged to you for the delicate way in which you have tried to inculcate better principles into us poor folks——"

But she was mistaken when she thought she could jest on such a subject, for her lip had quivered, and there was a pathetic ring in her voice as she brought the sentence to an abrupt close.   ·

·And now as it flashed upon him that his conduct must have appeared in the light of a deliberate insult, his face became the picture of remorse and mortification. Truly, a man is a blundering animal. But with not a little satisfaction she saw the perturbation of mind she had caused him, and, like the true woman that she was, came to his aid.

"Forgive me," she cried, and there was a hint of pity for him in her voice. "Do you think I am not a better judge of men than to suppose you guilty of such a thing. I saw from the first that you had not dreamed of preaching at us ; it was wrong of me to try and joke on such a subject. Come, let us cry quits, though your punishment has been more than you deserved." There was a strange mixture of contrition and generous frankness in her voice.

He could hardly trust himself to answer her on account of the unwonted elation that he felt. The girl began to show in a new aspect in his eyes. No experienced coquette of the gay up-to-date world could have applied the rack, and released him again, more skilfully that she had done. The very fact that she had caused him temporary pain made him feel attracted by her.

Then she rose from her seat, put on a dainty beaver cap, pulled on a large loose fur coat, and drew on her mitts.

He rose to go.

"Oh, no ; not till I come back," she said, pleasantly. "Jeannette will make some tea, and you must wait and have a cup with us. You see we are quite fashionable folk here, and generally have a cup in the afternoon about four o'clock ; but then we don't have it to dinner like most people in the North-West. I am going out to get some honey, which is in an underground cellar on the face of the butte, and won't be long. You see, it is my particular domain and not Jeannette's ; hers is in making the best cup of tea ever you drank. *Au revoir.*"

And with a graceful little curtsey that would have done credit to a court belle of the Second Empire and with a smile that seemed to banish care, she entered the little passage and passed out into the blizzard.

CHAPTER VIII.

"AN UNCOMMONLY BADLY FROZEN EAR."

MARIE ST. DENIS was back again in less than ten minutes. When she opened the outer door a gust of cold wind and a little cloud of fine powdery snow came in with her. Indeed, it was frozen on her eyelids and cheeks, and for a moment she was scarcely recognisable.

"The drifting snow stings and pricks one's face like so many needle points," she exclaimed, breathlessly.

"Pray come to the light," said Harry Yorke, taking her by the arm gently, and leading her to the window. "One of your ears looks as if it had been nipped by the frost."

And, truly enough, the lower lobe of one of her small shell-like ears was frozen; it was as white as the snow itself. Two minutes exposure to a sharp wind will often suffice to accomplish this not uncommon accident in these latitudes.

He took off her beaver cap gently, caught up a

small handful of snow which had crusted one side of her buffalo coat, and with one hand among the soft, gleaming tresses of her shapely head to steady it, with the other rubbed the nipped ear with snow. She submitted to the ordeal, as most people sooner or later learn to do in the North-West, as a matter of course, but with a somewhat heightened colour. Luckily, the frost-bite was a slight one, and, perhaps, the pain occasioned by the thawing-out process was inconsiderable, if, indeed, it pained at all. His prompt manipulation of the frozen lobe had minimised the unpleasant consequences usually attending such accidents.

But it was a remarkable thing that the operation took so much longer to perform than such operations usually do. Long after the ear had become a natural and healthy pink again—and she must have known very well that the frost had been driven out of it and the circulation of the blood restored—he continued clasping that beautiful head with one hand and rubbing that ear with the other. Her delicately flushed face and these bright eyes were dangerously near his then. Surely such a palpable dallying was a most reprehensible thing; but such things will be as long as human nature is human nature: as long as pretty girls will freeze their ears and there are accommodating young men handy to restore the suspended circulation.

Perhaps he had not thought himself capable of the

emotions that thrilled him when he felt the touch of
that silky hair and that cool, soft skin of hers. What
with that great pity with which he had begun to
regard her, and what with the knowledge of the
misery that he knew he must unwillingly have a
share in bringing upon her, she was exercising a
dangerous influence over him. Perhaps—and who
knows?—if old Jeannette had not been there he
might, for such things not infrequently happen—in
a moment of unreasoning and irresistible impulse
have caught her to him and told her how dear she
had become to him. He could remember how when
putting on the skates of the heiress in the Old
Country, the only feelings that he experienced when
he had handled her dainty little feet were that her
boots were uncommonly cold and clammy, and that
the steel sent an irresistible shiver through him. But
then, steel is not a beautiful thing like a pretty
girl's dainty ear. It was Jeannette that came
to the rescue of these two forgetful mortals just
then.

"*Allons-nous-en !*" she cried, "here is a cup of
beautiful tea with the best of cream in it. Bless my
heart, Marie, you must have had your ear very badly
frozen indeed, it takes such a long time to thaw
out!"

And the old lady chuckled grimly. In her youth
her own ears had been frozen many a time, and
thawed out too.

It was a significant thing that the rubbing should cease so suddenly, and that the pair should start apart so guiltily.

"Thank you very much," said the girl; "how it must have bored you to rub such a long time." She really meant nothing by this embarrassing speech; it was the only thing she could think of saying just then. People somehow will say things that they would like to have expressed differently on such occasions.

"Don't mention it," he replied, sheepishly. "It was an uncommonly badly frozen ear—I mean, I don't think that it was of much account after all."

"Oh, none whatever," she rejoined, simply and without thinking this speech in any way remarkable. But their eyes met, and there was a half-serious, laughing light in hers, and such a conscience-stricken look in his, that they both broke into a somewhat foolish and shamefaced laugh.

Then they sat in the early twilight and enjoyed Jeannette's tea. They did not drink it out of transparent china cups or chaste Sèvres, but out of plain, dead-white porcelain that is associated with the Hudson Bay Company's hardware department. And Jeannette poured it out of a little brown earthenware pot, of which the spout could hardly be said to be intact; but, so far as Harry Yorke was concerned, he only knew that it was most delicious tea, and that he could not help saying so. They sat

round the stove and chatted merrily, and under the
cheering influence of the tea, old Jeannette, with
the volatile spirits of her race, kept them amused
with some truly wonderful reminiscences she re-
counted. She possessed an almost inexhaustible
fund of the folk-lore of these once wild regions.
Of the days (not so very long ago, either) when the
buffalo blackened the plains with their numbers; of
the exciting adventures of the old French voyageurs
with the Indians; of the days of the old North-West
Company, and the Hudson Bay Company, when
Assiniboia, Manitoba and the Territories generally,
were unknown, or at least known only as part of the
"Great American Desert"; of the days of Louis
Riel and the first rebellion; reminiscences of
Wolseley; what Fort Garry looked like in the old
Red River days; and of the second rebellion. In
short, Jeannette was a living epitome of the history
of the Great Lone Land.

It grew dark, but still they sat talking and laughing; the cloud that threatened them had evidently
lifted for the time being. It would have been a
difficult thing for a stranger, seeing them sitting there,
to have guessed the nature of the business that
necessitated the presence of the police-sergeant in
that house. This individual, indeed, just then was
watching the effect of the flickering firelight as it
played upon the hair of Marie St. Denis, discovering
a gleam of gold in it. He would have been perfectly

content to sit there for an indefinite period, so satisfied was he with his occupation.

To the next room, where the officer, the private, and the scout sat, a peal of laughter had penetrated.

"What the devil's that?" suddenly cried the gentleman who represented Her Majesty. "I guess I he'rd that afore."

"Sir, did you do me the honour of addressing yourself to me?" inquired the little scout with gravity.

"Yess, stupid—I declare, Pierre, you grow stupider every day. I say you, constable, you Townley chap, what's that blanked row? It wasn't a horse, was it?" And Jamie's voice became tinged with anxiety.

"No, sir," was the reassuring answer of the private. "It is that beggar Yorkey—I beg your pardon, sir, I meant to say the sergeant, fooling with that pretty girl in the next room—and what a time he is having, to be sure!"

And at the thought of what he was losing, the outspoken and precocious youngster turned over on his side, and groaned.

"Is he—er—fond of that sort of thing?" queried the officer angling, according to his wont, for information of an incriminating nature.

"Well, I should just say, ra—ther," answered the private, somewhat unjustly it must be confessed, but with an excusable desire to punish his superior overcoming his scruples. "Why, Dick is such a confirmed flirt that he'd make love to the black-eyed goddess Night if he got the chance."

"You don't say so? The devil he would!" was the weak and dubious comment.

Jamie did not feel quite certain that the private's reply committed the sergeant to any specific charge, so did not care to pursue the matter further lest he should betray his ignorance as to the personality of the dark-eyed Eve in question, who, he concluded, might only be some Toronto barmaid, after all.

The private noted with disappointment that Jamie had refused the bait.

"It's my usual luck," he continued, forgetting the august presence of his superior officer in his half-envious soliloquy. "But who'd have thought that old Yorkey would have gone in for that sort of thing? He's a good-looking chap, though, with that independent, devil-may-care, cynical sort of air which some women like."

"Then why is it, *mon cher* Richard, you will not adopt some of these qualities you will make allusion to?" politely asked the little scout whose sharp ears had overheard the latter part of Dick Townley's meditations.

"Well, my dear Sancho," replied the youth, stroking the place where as yet any hirsute covering had resolutely refused to grow, much to the anxious one's disgust. "You see, it is not quite my style. I could not get up a Conrad-like appearance if I tried."

"Eh! what's that? What's that you say? More insolence, more rank insubordination and disrespectful talk of your superiors?" cried Jamie, who, with both ears very wide open, thought he had heard enough to justify him putting a charge against the private. "Just repeat that a-pop-probrious term."

(Jamie occasionally hunted his dictionary for long words, which he could use to advantage in the Orderly Room.)

"I said *Conrad-like*, sir," repeated the private, respectfully.

"And what the devil's that, sir? Is it a. man? Or, if it is a woman, which amounts to the same thing, who the devil is she?"—clearness of expression and a grammatical treatment of his personal pronouns were not Jamie's strong points.—"How dare you flaunt your blasphemous Cockney slang in my face? You he'rd him, Pierre? I call you as a witness."

And Jamie dived into a little valise to find his pencil and note-book.

"Hear what, sir? I didn't hear anything," said the scout stolidly. "Have you two been talking?"

"Oh, holy smoke and Jerusalem!" cried Jamie, springing to his feet. "This is a conspiracy—you two are in league—you've done nothing but insult me since we've been out. And you, Pierre, you'd tell me a barefaced, darned lie, you would!" And

Jamie's round face looked as if a glass of port had been poured over it.

" Sir," said the little scout, in turn getting warm and forgetting himself. "I would respectfully warn you to meditate just a leetle before you talk about lying—gentlemen do not do it ! "

"Well I'm——. There now, Townley, you heard that ; you can't say you didn't hear that blanked insolence ? " cried Jamie, running about distractedly, then stopping right in front of the private, who turned from the frosted window as if he had been looking out through it.

" Hear what, sir ?   Did you address me ? " and the private looked around with a face so stolid and stupid that it would have done credit to Jamie in one of his intellectual moods.   " Or were you talking to me, Pierre ?   I did not happen to be listening."

Jamie fairly staggered back against the wall speechless at this evidently barefaced conspiracy to set his authority at defiance.   The private and the scout really feared that the apoplectic fit which some day they knew must carry off Jamie was about to seize him just then, and were in no small degree alarmed.   To tell the truth, there was not one grain of disrespectful intention in either the private's or the scout's composition ; it was only in self-defence that they had to resort to these questionable means of evading the serious delinquencies which their ignorant superior would have involved them in, could he have had his own way. Jamie staggered to the door, and went into the passage.

"Well, I'm blest!" said the private under his breath. "Some of the officers in the North-West Mounted Police are the best friends some of the rank and file can have, and, of course, the Canadian Government are at liberty to pursue their own policy; but when their policy necessitates the granting of commissions to cads and tyrants like Jamie, I think it is time for all respectable men to leave the force. I wish to goodness I could scrape enough money together to buy my discharge."

In the meantime the officer had gone to the door of the next room and kicked violently upon it.

"Hilloa, there, Yorke!" he shouted—Jamie usually affected a nasal drawl. "Darn you, Yorke! come here; I want you. What do you mean fooling away your time for with that wench? I want you to come and put Townley under arrest for rank insubordination, using insolent language to his superiors, and making a false statement. I'll get 'Hatchet-face'"—which, by the way, was a nick-name given by the half-breeds to a superintendent commanding the division—"to imprison him, and risk an appeal."

On hearing this excited speech the sergeant flushed angrily and sprang to his feet. Jeannette stepped to the stove, and seized a dipper of boiling water. The beautiful "wench" referred to cried mischievously, "Come in."

But the old adage, "once bitten, twice shy," held good in Jamie's case.

"Not if I knows it! Oh, not for Joseph!" was the drawling reply to this invitation from behind the door. "I'm too fly by long odds for that. I don't come in as long as that old she-cat has that dipper of water handy on the stove."—Jamie had wisely reconnoitred through the keyhole.—"Get a rustle on there, Yorke, or I'll shove a charge against you."

The sergeant hurried into the passage so as not to keep his superior officer waiting.

"Come outside into the stable," said Jamie. "I want to talk to you. What? You want to put your fur coat on, do you? Oh, never mind, I'm wrapped up sufficiently for both of us"—his characteristic wit was of a light and playful turn—"I declare, Yorke, you're getting more of a tenderfoot every day. I say, by the way, don't you think you're rushing that girl in there rather too hard? You want to look out and not scare her at the start off ; give her 'head' a little at first ; then just let her feel the bit, and stay with it until you've got her well in hand—young women are like young horses : they want a bit of jockeyin'."

Harry Yorke did not dispute the correctness of this analagous equine treatment. It was a subject which he did not care about discussing, least of any man, with his superior officer. He led the way into the stable, and then waited to hear what the officer had to say. It took some considerable time to say, and considerable ingenuity on the sergeant's part to piece together the many obscure and irrelevant things that were said, so as to arrive at a fairly intelligible idea of what had occurred. And while the sergeant was pointing out to him the futility attending the putting of the private under arrest, if the latter and the scout insisted on maintaining that they had simply misunderstood him, he, the inspector, true to the promptings of his erratic mind, went on to speak of another phase of the situation.

" Now, then," he said ; " it's time this blizzard was lifting. It might lift at any time now ; and more than likely Gabriel St. Denis ain't far off. He'll probably take a look in here to see how the little wench is getting on afore he proceeds to the Hat with his cargo of liquor. The snow will make travelling for a waggon rather difficult ; but, at any rate, ther'll be no difficulty in tracking anything supposing we shouldn't catch sight of them just at first, or should even pass them and then come across their tracks travelling northwards. By the way, I think it would be just as well to keep an eye on them women to-morrow. They might mount one o' them cayuses after we're gone, cut down one o' them coullees, get ahead of us, and give old St. Denis the tip. I've he'rd tell o' woman do that sort o' thing afore. But, anyhow, no woman's game to do it unless in broad daylight. But we'll watch them.

I've some experience o' women. Oh, I'm up to their little games, you kin bet your sweet-scented socks ! "

As the sergeant had not the slightest inclination to dispute this point either with his superior, he muttered something which might mean anything, but did not feel particularly at ease in his own mind. Jamie looked around the stable with an air of satisfaction ; then, as if a new idea had just presented itself to his mind, he said, with unction—

" I say, Yorke, ain't a stable a stunnin' place to spend one's time in ?   I'm darned if I couldn't live in one ! "

With this sentiment the sergeant hastened to agree.   It also struck him with a certain whimsical force that Nature did occasionally do unaccountable things.   When, for instance, she gave some brutes — notably the horse and dog — noble traits that would have distinguished them as human beings, and gave some human being predilections that would have distinguished them as brutes.   Then he felt in an apologetic frame of mind towards the brutes for having, even in imagination, added such an unworthy specimen to their number.

Then dark-winged Night, that witching, dreamy-eyed goddess, came fluttering down over the blizzard-haunted, lonely land, shadowing the snow-blurred landscape.   Looking out upon such a hopelessly dreary scene one could hardly imagine that the sun

would ever shine upon it again : that the cutting
and icy air would ever again be mild and balmy :
that the songs of birds would rise in it, and that
trees and flowers would blossom and bloom there,
such a grip had the Ice-king on it then. It was
hard to realise that, on the other side of that wild
storm-cloud, the placid moon and stars looked down
as serenely beautiful and immutable as ever, just as
they had looked down for countless ages, through
realms of space, with sphinx-like inscrutability upon
this little planet of ours.

CHAPTER IX.

WHAT A GIRL WILL DO.

MIDNIGHT: and Sleep, that gracious goddess wearing the pathetic image of her twin sister Death, folding one half of a weary world in her fond embrace. Midnight: and a change has come over the spirit of the elements. For, as if the vacuum to which the snow-laden air hurried northwards had been filled, the blizzard gradually ceased to blow, and sighed itself to rest. And then a stillness, and a peace, as profound as that which is supposed to brood over a dead lunar landscape, fell upon the ghastly and desolate face of this great, lone, snow-shrouded prairie-land. As if a curtain had been drawn away from between heaven and earth, the eternal dome of heaven showed clearly overhead. It was gemmed and lit up by countless myriads of God's own light-givers.

And yet there are those who will look upon such a sight, who may even comprehend the marvellously adjusted system that maintains the harmony of the spheres in illimitable space, and will doubt the existence of a Divine Intelligence to have planned it so. There are those who, because their speculative minds have wandered and lost themselves in the cloudlands of metaphysics and transcendentalism, will say with querulous and pitiable self-sufficiency, " There is no God," and at the same time lose sight of the significant fact and reason of their own existence. There are those sterner ones, who, grappling with this fact, think that they have solved the whole mystery of life by a purely temporal theory of evolution—a pitiful theory when standing alone, when all it can teach is that Man has raised himself a little higher than the brutes, and, like them, has no life beyond the grave. Gross, cheerless, and pernicious philosophy, antagonistical to the practical ethics of progress—God's own way of working. Whether we have been evolved or not is, perhaps, a matter of little moment after all. Let us admit evolution, which is likely enough, not regarding it with a cold, materialistic, and inadequate philosophy, but with that higher reason that He has implanted in our breasts. Then, is not His way of working only the more wonderful and sublime, the juster—more intelligible—subtler—more comprehensive, the surer system of government when it distinguishes between responsible and irresponsible Man? Man of no consequence, forsooth ! when it has taken who knows what æons to make him what he is—

8

a being whose sense of right and wrong has outgrown the mere judicial phase—that phase in accordance with Man's purely temporal well-being.

Surely this thought, then, should give us courage, and enable us to cope with these devils Doubt and Despair. Seeing that all things in nature bear the impress of intelligent design and progression; since death itself is but the attainment of another rung in the ladder that reaches to a fuller life, we, therefore, who have become *responsible* beings, do not tarry here, but journey on to reap as we have sown, in that Hereafter so wisely shrouded from us.

Are not our lives greatly trials of faith? for can the philosopher see farther behind the scenes than the child? Trials of faith, but with the abundant proofs of His handiwork—the finger of God pointing onwards, upwards, and appealing to our truer selves.

Twelve o'clock: and in a little end room of the house Marie St. Denis has risen from the bed on which she had a few hours earlier flung herself without having undressed. She struck a light stealthily, lit a candle, and listened intently. There is no sound to be heard save the hard, metallic ticking of the old clock in the kitchen, and the occasional muffled bark and stifled yelps of the hound as it lies dreaming in front of the kitchen stove. A dog's actual life is not such a very short one after all, for he lives every minute of his waking life, and he lives his

sleeping one as well—in his dreams. Occasionally
the girl could hear—so still it had become—the occasional stirring of the cattle in the corral and shed.
The horses by this time were lying down, or dozing
and nodding like sleepy human beings, in their stalls.
Then an energetic young cock in the partially underground hen-house hard by, having been awakened by
a shaft of moonlight streaming full in upon him,
suddenly straightened himself and began to crow
lustily, under the delusion that he had overslept himself, and that he had allowed humanity in general to
sleep longer than that time which it was his privilege
to apportion for it. There are many men in the
world who resemble the cock ; they think they are
brought expressly into it by an intelligent Providence
in order to make their own particular presence known,
and direct their neighbours' affairs.

The girl placed the light in a shaded corner of
the room, and looked out of the little window.
Well might she start ; the blizzard had utterly ceased,
and outside it was almost as clear as day, for there
was a bright three-quarter moon. The time had come
for action now ; but could she leave the house without being observed ? She must not, in the first place,
awaken Jeannette, who might try to detain her. The
sergeant had promised that he would not interfere
with her actions ; but it was just possible that if any
of the others happened to be awake, and looked out,
they would see that the storm had ceased—even if the

humming of the stove did not prevent them from
marking the absence of the wind—and at once be on
the alert to look out for her father, who, they knew,
if he were not even now near at hand, must be
travelling again. It was the fixed resolve of this
daughter of the prairie, to go out alone upon it, and
meeting her father, apprise him of the proximity of
the police, and so enable him to escape the danger,
either by cacheing the liquor and returning empty-
handed, or by another scheme which her fertile brain
had already conceived. She knew it was bitterly
cold outside, but she had not lived in that country the
greater part of her life not to know exactly how to
prepare for such an emergency.

She slipped on a pair of extra woollen sox, and
a pair of moccasins, put on a species of buckskin
legging, beautifully fringed, and wrought with coloured
silks, such as some women have worn in the Western
States. She invested herself in a light and similarly
wrought loose garment, resembling a buckskin shirt,
and wound round her waist a long silk sash. She
pulled a large silky beaver cap down over her ears,
pulled on a pair of beaver mitts, then drew from
under the bed a pair of snowshoes, and carried them
under one arm, ready to slip on her feet. She was a
picturesque and typical figure for a land of ice and
snow. Then, as stealthily, she extinguished the light,
and left the room. So softly did she step that even
old Michelle, the hound, who lay before the stove, did

not hear her footsteps, he only stirred uneasily in his sleep, pawed the air wildly for a minute or two with his forepaws, and gave a few sharp, but muffled yelps. He was in full chase after a coyote ; and now he was squaring old accounts with it.

Then, as noiselessly as a thief in the night, she prepared to leave the house. She stood for a moment in the little passage, and with every sense quickened, listened intently. If any one were to awake now, and discover her presence, then all her scheming would be at an end, and the ruin of her father would be accomplished. Her heart throbbed wildly, she could almost hear it beat, and for a moment a sickening fear took possession of her as she heard some one stir in the next room, and a voice with a nasal drawl in it quaver out—

" I say, Yorke—darn you, Yorke ! By Jimini ! the beggar sleeps as soundly as if he was a gentleman with nothing on his mind ! Show a leg ! I he'rd them horses just now, an' I'm afeard one of them must have got its leg over the halter and be hanging hisself. Get a blanked rustle on, an' see to it."

" Very good, sir," answered the sleepy Yorke. " But I think it is unlikely ; I tied the horses up myself last evening, and short, too. But we'll see."

In point of fact Jamie had heard nothing, but having taken an extra heavy supper, was unable to sleep ; and, thinking it was a pity that others should sleep when he could not, decided to rouse up the sergeant. He had half a mind to wake the other two.

The poor girl heard no more. Silently she opened the door and passed out into the night.

The sergeant arose, and tying on his moccasins left the room quietly, so as not to disturb the others. When he opened the door he was not a little surprised at the change—the beauty and serenity of the night. The whole world seemed flooded with a silvery, mystic moonlight. He was passing the gable end of the house when he suddenly caught sight of an upright, dark form that showed imperfectly in the shadow. His first impulse was to challenge it after the manner of a sentry ; but an undefined something kept him silent. Still the figure did not move, and still he did not know what it was. Then that unaccountable spirit of curiosity which so often exerts such a strange power over us—perhaps more noticeable in the case of animals—even in the face of danger, possessed him, and he took a step or two towards it. It was a human being. As if some sudden intuitive sense had enlightened him, he went right up to this person, and gently taking an arm, led him, or her, forward, so that the bright moonlight might fall full upon the face. But before he did this he got a glimpse of a woman's skirt. Still the figure did not utter a word. He did, and it was a very prosaic exclamation indeed —" By Jove !"

And the fearless and beautiful face of Marie St.

Denis, with her soft, expressive eyes, now strangely bright, looked questioningly into his as he placed his two hands instinctively on her shoulders, so as to steady her face, and see who it was. She looked like some spirit of the night in that dreary solitude, haunting the little speck of civilisation, so silent was she and so unearthly her beauty seemed with the pale moonlight playing on it. Then she drew one hand from a beaver mitt, and placed one slender finger upon her lips. He interpreted the action. For a minute—only for a minute—a painful warfare raged within this man—duty, and something that he would not admit to himself, but at the same time which was very nearly akin to love. But what right had he to control her actions? Besides, had he not given her his word that he would not do so? Again, was he doing right in allowing this girl to go out alone upon the coullee-scarred and treacherous prairie, on to what might be death? But what was he, again, that he should constitute himself her mentor? As if it cost him a struggle to do it, he took his hands from off her shoulders. Turning abruptly, and with what might have been a curse or a blessing on his trembling lips, he left her without another word.

When he reached the stable door he turned to look after her ; but she had vanished as completely as if she had been one of those beautiful fabled spirits of the night whom she so much resembled.

CHAPTER X.

A TERRIBLE TIME.

IF it had cost Harry Yorke a mental struggle to let Marie St. Denis go as he did, he did not know that she who was the subject of it, with her quick, intuitive sense, fully realised the seriousness of that struggle, and suffered, doubtless, as keenly as he did himself. For the sergeant knew that in allowing her to go he had voluntarily relinquished that career in which he had distinguished himself, and through which he had hoped to rise in Her Majesty's service. He felt himself dishonoured in his own eyes. He felt—so palpable a thing was his sense of duty—that he was acting treacherously to that officer under whose command he now was. He did not try to soothe his conscience, as many of his comrades might have done, by telling himself that the brutal and demoralising conduct of this officer was such that many good men who had entered the force with the determination to walk straight and rise in it had become so disheartened, and their sense of duty so perverted, that

to disobey this officer's often questionable commands
was neither considered a disgrace nor breach of duty.
It was not the mere loss in a worldly sense that
troubled him ; this disregard of himself was indeed
what had kept him a comparatively poor man. He
did not attempt to defend his conduct by telling himself that he had sacrificed his career for his great pity
for her—which, indeed, was partly the case—for in
his conduct he was conscious of a feeling which, if it
did not altogether partake of that which some men
call "the unselfishness of love," still did not justify
him in acting as he did. For he knew that allowing
her to go meant that she would in all probability meet
with her father and warn him of the presence of the
police, defeat the ends of justice, and bring discredit
on himself. It meant that when his term of service
had expired, in a few months from then, he must look
out for some other employment: he could not remain
in a force that he could not be faithful to. He had
a little money ; by working hard, and with economy,
he might even be in a position to start ranching in a
humble way. At times he told himself that he was
a fool, and asked himself what this girl was to him.
If she had entertained any respect or thought for
him, would she have asked him to as good as sacrifice
himself for her ? But when he thought of a frail girl
going out alone at midnight upon the bleak and
blizzard-haunted prairie, where death might spring
up and claim her at any moment, with the faint hope

of warning an erring father from his danger, he felt that to thwart such a noble if natural deed were a crime that more than outweighed all other considerations. No, he was human, but he would again do as he had done if he had occasion to. Yes, even if he knew—and, when he came to think of it, she had given him no sign either one way or another—he were nothing to her, and, admitting himself in love with her, he were pursuing an ignis-fatuus.

As for Marie St. Denis, if she thought at all about the risk she was running in going out as she did upon the prairie alone, it was now swallowed up in weightier considerations. True, she knew something of the treacherous nature of the blizzard—how for a while it will die away, and the sun or moon will shine out brightly again, only to be suddenly obscured as the treacherous, snow-laden wind swoops down, like a bird of prey, to seize its hapless victim unawares. She remembered how, only last winter, a Mounted Policeman had been caught thus—how he had wandered round about in that fatal and mysterious circle, until the stinging, icy blast proved too much for him; and with the waning of hope came that wavering of mind and irresponsibility over one's own actions which, let us believe, God sends in His mercy. . . . When his frozen body had been found, some days afterwards, there was a bullet-wound in his head and a discharged pistol by his side. He had anticipated Death. Though Marie was no fatalist, she was

only a woman who was as sensitive as any other
to the terrors that encompass death, and the mysterious unseen world; but she was a heroine in the
truest sense of the word, in that she did not hesitate
to brave death and its terrors so that she might
perform faithfully what she considered her duty.
There was only one thing that troubled her; and the
more she thought of it, the more she saw that in her
anxiety to save her father she had imposed a sacrifice on another. She was now painfully alive to the
fact that, in his chivalrous desire to serve her, Harry
Yorke had sacrificed his worldly career, and, what
was doubtless dearer to him, his own sense of honour
and duty. Why had she asked him to compromise
that sense of honour? Could she not have simply
left the possibility of his non-interference to that
vague but oft-times favourable influence men call
"Chance," and thus have saved him? She knew
that he was a man looked up to and respected by
all ranks in his calling; but that, in asking him to
do as he had done, she had withdrawn from him
that chance which might have led to his promotion.
Had this been all, it were bad enough; but she
instinctively recognised that this man valued something more highly than worldly gain—his own
honour. How could she, she asked herself, who
was only a poor obscure girl, have asked him, who
had been on terms of intimacy with women belonging
to that other great outside world, to do this thing?

For, though feeling she had much in common with
this man, she had looked upon him as superior to
herself and apart from her life, even though he belonged only to the rank and file of the North-West
Mounted Police. If pity, as they say, is akin to love,
then Marie St. Denis was in a dangerous way. But
the thought of that father, whom she loved with an
intensity that paled all other considerations, governed
her actions then. With a beating heart, and a mind
that was swayed by conflicting emotions, but in which
there was still a dominant one, she set out on her
errand.

And now she hurried on her dangerous way. For
a mile or so she kept, as best she could, to the long,
narrow, rib-like patches of exposed ground which the
wind had kept clear of the snow, near the banks of
the creek. Occasionally she would spring from one
rib to another ; her idea was to cause the police some
difficulty in finding her tracks when they missed her
in the morning, when she knew the first thing they
would think of doing would be to follow her up.
Considering how long the blizzard had lasted there
was no very great depth of snow, save in the drifts ;
for it is not the actual quantity of snow which falls
that constitutes a blizzard, but the rate at which the
snow that does fall is hurried along and kept continually in a state of motion by the fierce gale. Perhaps
a blizzard resembles nothing so much as a sand-storm
in the desert. She had the satisfaction of remembering

that a man like her father, who knew the prairie so well, would have no great difficulty in finding ground comparatively free from snow on which he could travel with the waggons. Then she left the prairie and made over to the creek, and there slipped her feet into the buckskin laces of the snowshoes. It was a species of locomotion at which she was an adept ; for often had she indulged in long, solitary walks thus in the winter-time. This, perhaps, helped to account for the purity of that wonderful complexion of hers. A keen frost had set in, and there was a stillness as of death over that ghastly and shimmering moonlit land. She followed the course of the creek ; for the first two miles she knew every foot of the way, and, therefore, could avoid the crevasses that intersected the cut-banks. She knew exactly the route her father would adopt coming back from Montana ; and her idea had been to turn him back into United States territory before the police could catch up on him. But she had no premonition that the Fates had decreed otherwise. In order to cause the police delay when they eventually found her tracks, she crossed and recrossed the creek at certain places where she knew the snow lay many feet deep underneath. (Loudly did the over-eager officer of Mounted Police curse those treacherous pitfalls on the morrow.) She wound in and out amongst the thick clumps of willow and elder. They would have their work cut out for them who followed in her tracks. She was only human after all, and she could not help laughing silently to herself at times when, with vivid imagination, she pictured the inspector floundering about on his horse in one of these deep snowdrifts—perhaps nothing but his moonlike face visible above the surface. When she thought of the use he would put that unique vocabulary of his to, and the number of new and choice words and expressions which he would coin for such occasions, she had actually to stop to repress the fit of laughter that would fain have shaken her. But, at times, she would experience twinges of conscience when she asked herself if it were right to create delays which might imperil the lives of those who had sacrificed so much to help her. When she contemplated such disastrous contingencies there was an almost pitiful look of terror on her face that would doubtless have surprised her prospective victims, could they have seen it. At such times she thought herself a very wicked creature indeed. Perhaps, there was a considerable spark of old Mother Eve in her after all. But the thought of her father would gradually overcome her scruples, and she would push on again.

She began to realise she had travelled some considerable distance, and was feeling tired. She sat down on a rising piece of ground and looked around. What a weird, unearthly landscape showed up all around her ! She could follow the dark, uncertain line of the creek, as it wandered, in an erratic sort of

fashion, away into that mystic and shadowy landscape, until it was lost in dim obscurity. But tower-
ing, as it were, into that starlit other world, she could
see the three conical peaks of the Sweet Grass Hills
looking down upon that spectral land beneath them.
They seemed very beautiful and grand, very solemn
and majestic. There must have been in Marie St.
Denis' nature that susceptibility to what is beautiful
in Nature—that responsive note which indicates that
the soul is capable of receiving those deeper and
sublimer lessons from God's own handiwork. As she
looked upon these snow-clad peaks soaring heaven-
wards, her whole being was stirred with a sense of
the eternal, and the majesty of that Presence which
created all things. For a brief space the very sight
of these hills seemed to give her fresh strength and
courage. But, alas! tired Nature would reassert
herself. It was the old story of the willing spirit
and the weak flesh. For two nights she had not
slept a wink. Hope had buoyed her up; but, as
stern reality dispelled hope, the reaction of her
physical body set in; and subtly and mercifully was
the change brought about. She began to be conscious, at times, of being the victim of her own
fancies.

And now she came to a place where she had to
push through a deep, narrow gorge, which opened
out into an amphitheatre-like space where there was
a thicket of cotton-wood trees, and which had been

used in the old days as a burying ground for the
Indians.   It was a horrible place, and even this
healthy, prairie-bred girl experienced that sense of
awe and fear which will steal over one—unless one
is dead to all human emotions—when one is in the
presence of relics of mortality.   This little valley,
surrounded by high banks, had an evil reputation.
Some renegade Sioux or Piegan Indians had some
few years before committed some bloody atrocities
near this spot, and the dead had been buried here.
Upon rude platforms were ranged human bodies
wrapped in buffalo robes and blankets, which were
now coated and crusted with drifting snow.   The
great gaunt, scraggy branches of the leafless trees,
and that significant scaffolding with its awful burdens,
when viewed from the frozen bed of the creek on
which she walked, stood out with a horrible distinct-
ness against the star-lit sky.   Time, or the bears,
had broken down some of these stages, and she knew
that hideous, shapeless and unnameable things lay
strewn around and partially buried in the snow.   It
was a veritable Golgotha.   And now a cold shiver
ran through the frame of the girl as she lifted her
eyes and gazed fearfully up at a number of grinning
skulls which a playful Mounted Policeman, or wandering cowboy of a decorative turn of mind, had fixed
on the scraggy limb of a gaunt and blasted oak tree.
Even as the girl looked there rose a weird, eerie
moan on the still night, and a startling crash that

drove the blood to her heart, and chilled the surface of her body. In spite of herself she sank down on her knees, and clasping her hands before her, muttered a prayer as best she could. Marie was not naturally timid ; but that place had an evil reputation, and the law of association is a powerful thing. But it was only a stray breath of wind, straying down the gorge, that had caused the moaning ; and the weight of the snow upon one of these awful burdens had been too much for the rotten supports, and had borne it with a crash to the ground. For a moment she felt as if her strength had deserted her ; she was left weak and trembling. But the thought of her father and the danger he was in came to her aid ; tremblingly she rose from the snow-covered ice and went on again, but with weary steps.

It grew colder and colder, the thermometer must have dropped to at least 20° below zero, and King Frost was doing his best, or worst, to paralyse every living thing. But still Marie could not be said to suffer from cold ; she only began to feel strangely drowsy and at times caught herself walking in an almost trance-like state. That subtle and fatal land of forgetfulness, which she knew was exercising its potent spell over her, aroused her to renewed exertion. At last she passed out of that loathsome valley where the high ground ceased, and stood once more upon the banks of the creek on the rolling prairie.

And now, with heavy and ever weakening steps,

9

the girl ascended a little ridge where she could get a
good view of the surrounding country. But as far as
the eye could penetrate in that clear moonlight there
was nothing in sight. She had told herself that at
this point she must necessarily see some signs of her
father's approach with the teams, and that hope had
buoyed her up till then. She was bitterly disappointed. She had walked for several miles, and now
what was she to do? Could she go back without
having seen her father, and listen to the low-minded
taunts of the Mounted Police officer? Or would she
wait there, in the hope that her father might soon
come up; running the risk of that insidious death-
sleep, which even then threatened her? As for going
back: when she came to think of it, she felt utterly
unable for the task. And now the real nature of
Marie began to show itself. She hardly for a moment
thought of that fate which might so soon overtake
her. She had none of that enervating, half-pitying
compassion for herself in the abstract that some less
unselfish ones have. She did not even regret the
step she had taken, though it now threatened her life.
She only knew that if she had not come on this vain
errand she would have regretted the staying behind
still more. Her only thoughts were for her father ;
but as her eyes wandered over the ghastly prospect,
her heart sank within her.

At last, in the east, the grey dawn was breaking ;
the stars began to disappear, one by one, like lights

in a great city at break of day. A thin, ghost-like mist began to creep from butte to coullee across the billowy prairie, like the phantom sea that it was. It hung low, and converted the tops of the little buttes and ridges into mimic islands, until the earth somewhat resembled one of those landscapes that the imaginative mind will conjure up in the clouds. But, away to the left, a couple of miles off, the girl saw a unique sight. She saw the entrance to the Devil's Playground : that weird, nightmarish valley, into which the boldest Indian will not enter, but only gaze upon fearfully from the brink of the chasm. Constituting the portals of this valley, the girl saw gigantic pillar-like masses of vitrified clay that resembled the painted pillars in some vast gorgeous and barbaric old-world temple. Indeed, the variety and originality of colouring in these pillars was beautiful if bewildering in effect. Just beyond them lurked, reproduced in coloured clays, these wonderful freaks of Nature : the forms of monstrous and grotesque animals, whose shapes startled one with a suggestion of intelligent design. From the painted and garish terraces themselves projected griffins and gargoyles, just as one sees them in old and quaint cathedrals, but only more grotesque and suggestive by reason of their vivid colouring.

The girl looked longingly towards the portals of this valley of freaks ; but she could see no sign of any living thing near them. She had thought that the smugglers might have taken shelter there from the fury of the blizzard. But had they done so she thought that, by this time, they would have begun their journey again so as to pass the police lines ere the sun rose. "Oh, father, father!" she cried, and the unbidden tears started to her eyes.

Then her brain, or old King Death, played her a strange trick. But not by any means an unusual one. For those who have been in the very jaws of death, and have been snatched back, can tell some marvellous tales. Marvellous because they are utterly foreign to our preconceived notions of the King of Terrors. Especially can those who have passed the Rubicon—the painful stage of mental and physical suffering—and whose feet have trod the mystic threshold of the Unknown : whether they are lost ones on the African desert, in the Australian bush, castaways at sea, or the vanquished victims of some fell disease. It is, indeed, a merciful thing, and shows how wonderfully and fearfully we are made, to think that the brain comes eventually to our aid, to take somewhat away from the agony of death, and rob it, as it were, of some of the terror it would fain inspire. So now with Marie St. Denis ; for gradually there stole a wonderful peace of mind—something that almost approached a physical glow over her ; the present with its horror passed utterly away, and this was the vision she had in its stead :—

It was a bright summer's day ; the prairie was gay

and beautiful with its very brightest carpet of green,
and its choicest display of wild flowers. There were
the lilies that outshone the glory of Solomon, and the
pink and clustering roses that glowed as must have
done the roses of Sharon to have made their beauty
scriptural. There were the nodding sunflowers
winking in the gentle breeze, like so many eyes of
fire, the blue larkspurs, the yellow and purple violets,
blue bells and a hundred other flowers, perhaps as
beautiful, but not so familiar as these more common
ones. No wonder they say that on the prairie there
is a flower for every day in the year. Close to the
trail a great waggon is camped, with a white canvas
top to it. Some little distance off the horses, released
from their toil, are rolling in the grass and throwing
their legs wildly into the air in the most grotesque
and extravagant fashion, in their endeavour to roll
from one side to another. And she is crawling about
on the grass, with one hand grasping the gathered
skirt that holds the flowers she has been plucking.
Close to her, on his hands and knees like a great
overgrown school-boy, is her father, with smiles
wreathing that usually sad and austere face. She
had made him stoop down before her, and like the
playful child she is, she has stuck a fringe of flowers
into the band of his broad cow-boy hat, and is now
endeavouring to string a chain of daisies round his
neck. All the children of Eve pursue the same
methods of play the world over. And this grave,

bearded man is looking as proud of that chain as if
it were of gold, and she were the heir to the throne
decorating him.   As proud ?—prouder by far! for
there is no pride on earth to compare to that of a
father in his only child.   She is happy as the day is
long.   Ay, long—but never too long for them !

Then a sudden shock, and her dream shivered.
She had slipped back into a recumbent position on
the snow, and the sudden movement roused her for
a brief spell.   With a lightning-like flash the brain
realised the danger of the situation, and urged the
weakened body to renewed exertion.   But it was
powerless to respond.

Was this, then, the end of her young life?—she,
who had cherished such dreams and hopes of the
future.   Was she to perish like one of the beasts of
the field, on that desolate snow-bound ridge ?   Were
the birds of the air, and the jackals of the plain—the
prairie and timber wolves—to fight over her poor
body ?   A thing so fair as she were rare prey for
such evil-looking brutes as wolves.   Even now, far
off, but ever drawing nearer, she heard a mournful
and prolonged eerie cry, and she knew that already
a wolf was upon her tracks.   She had a small revolver
on her belt ; but, perhaps, it was not worth while
using it.   Poor Marie, well might she pray ; for that
sleep which means death was very close upon her
now.

And then rose up before her that face that had so

often smiled upon her in her dreams, and she knew it
was her mother's face, that dear mother whom she
had lost so long ago that her image had become but
a sacred memory. Then the face of her father, that
face so full of simple tenderness, seemed to look
down upon her, and a struggling gleam of semi-
consciousness shook her for a few minutes with a
tempest of agony, as she pictured him all alone in
the world, without any one to love—without any one
to strengthen or care for him, and with only the
memory of a fitfully sunny past behind him. Surely
this was the agony and sting of death.

Death !—she must rouse herself. It was a sinful
thing to let death steal upon her with its subtle
visions and lethargy ! She would break the spell;
if she died it would be upon her feet. But, horror!
the muscles of her body refused to obey the commands of the brain. She could not move !

But just before the mists lifted before the rays of
that wintry sun she seemed to hear, as if in the air,
but wonderfully clearly and distinctly, that majestic
and triumphant song of adoration, the Hallelujah
Chorus. She had heard it in the convent : it had
haunted her since, and now it came as if to lighten
her end. She ˉheard myriads of voices—beautiful
voices : the silvery voices of women, the voices of
boys, and the resonant and maturer voices of man-
hood, blend together with the pealing notes of the
King of Instruments, until they spoke as one in

harmonious concord : with a sweetness that ravished her senses, and permeated her whole being.

"*Hallelujah ! For the Lord God omnipotent reign-eth !*" they all cried together, with one mighty and resonant volume of sound : with one joyous burst of triumph and of gladness.   And the basses heralding the clarion-like voices of the sopranos sang, "*And He shall reign for ever and ever.*"

Then the tenors and the basses cried "*Hallelujah ! Hallelujah!*"   The silvery altos, and the mellow con-traltos glided into the ever-growing melody with— "*for ever, and ever, King of Kings, and Lord of Lords.*"

And that mighty, fugual, soul-stirring chorus rolled on ; the beautiful lights and shades of the theme pursuing, meeting, and crossing one another trans-versely like the shafts of pearly, silvery and rosy light, that play upon the face of the Aurora under a Northern sky.   It was many-throated, many tongued, but with one soul only.   It was a mosaic of sound—the voice of the Creator speaking through the creature.

It was a glorious Pæan—a fitting death hymn for one so young and beautiful.

And now, ere that insidious death-sleep dulled her wandering senses—robbing her even of that land of dreams and shadows, and ere her eyelids closed over the wells of liquid light, she heard these words so full of a divine promise—

"*And tho' worms destroy this body, yet in my flesh shall I see God.*"

Surely the angels of Light were bending over her then—so fair and peaceful her young face seemed, and hid the grim shadow of the Angel of Death as he hovered over her.

"*But, thanks be to God, who giveth us the Victory,*" chanted all the voices together.

The lemon-glow that trembled in the east died at the sun's first kiss. A blush, as subtle as the tender red that dyes a maiden's cheek, spread over earth and sky. The stars grew dim, and blended with the blue. The grey mists lifted from the spectral earth. That dream of glory round the Ice-king's throne shivered—the way of dreams.

And then the girl slept.

CHAPTER XI.

"GET ON HER TRAIL, PIERRE."

WHEN Harry Yorke, the police sergeant, had gone to the stable when ordered to do so by his superior officer, he found that all the horses were lying down in their stalls, peacefully dozing like so many respectable human beings. Jamie had said that he heard them pounding the cobble-stones violently ; but as the floor happened to be a mud one, it is only charitable to suppose that the officer must have forgotten this fact, and that his imagination must have been uncommonly active. He waited in the stable for some little time, and then went back to the room where his comrades were. According to his instructions he told the inspector that the blizzard had ceased. As he had expected, the latter gave him some fresh orders.

"Then, open the door," said the humanitarian, "and wake up Townley and Pierre, and the three of you keep a sharp look out on the opposite door, so that none of these women can pass out without you seeing them. Keep pinching the third man so that you will be able to keep awake."

A fool may have humour which wise men may laugh over, but the wit of the cruel and crafty is like a nettle, it has a sting for all. The hand that crushes is the proper one to handle it.

The sergeant reluctantly did as he was ordered ; the three watchers, putting some fresh fuel on the fire, began their weary vigil, and Jamie began to snore.

All inclination to sleep had been effectually banished from the sergeant's eyes. How could he sleep with the thought of that poor girl out upon the snow-bound prairie ? At times it was very noticeable to the other two watchers that he betrayed considerable impatience as the night, or rather the morning, wore on. Sometimes he got up, and silently paced the hut —the officer was now sound asleep—and once or twice he went out and, opening the outer door, looked into the semi-darkness and listened. Towards morning, as if his impatience impelled him to action, he went out into the stable and remained there about an hour. On coming in again, a gust of cold air, like a tangible presence and which cut like a knife, came in with him, and awoke Jamie.

" The deuce "—only he put it more forcibly—" take you, Yorke ; were you born in a barn ? " snapped the Amiable One.

" Daylight is coming, sir," said the sergeant, ignoring his superior's polite request for information.

"It's coming, is it?" cried Jamie, irritably, and it is only charitable to say, half awake. "Well, then, let it come, and be d——d to it!"

At this slightly irrelevant but characteristic speech, that was delivered in a thick and incoherent voice, which a man who had been having more to drink than was good for him might adopt, the scout, in spite of himself, broke into a loud succession of snorts which sounded suspiciously.

"What the devil's the matter with you now, Pierre?" asked Jamie, querulously. "Got an attack of the colic?"

"Yes, sir," answered Pierre, gravely. He had just managed to check himself. "And it is a maladie terrible, and will many times occasion me considerable distress. The worst of it is, it will proceed for me at such odd times."

"Humph! Horses fed?" asked Jamie.

"Yes, sir; and stables cleaned out," answered the sergeant.

The private and the scout exchanged glances; but as it was no uncommon thing in the police force for non-commissioned officers to turn their hands to, on occasions, they thought no more about it.

Just then there came a knock at the door, and the voice of old Jeannette was heard inquiring for the sergeant. She asked the latter if he would come into the kitchen for a minute, as she wished to speak to him. The sergeant hastened to grant her request.

Jeannette, who was considerably agitated, turned to him and spoke as soon as he entered the kitchen.

"My Marie," she said, "she has gone through the night—do you think there is any danger? Ah! I see you know of it. Why did you let her go? She may perish. Fool that I was not to know she would try it as soon as the blizzard went down. But it may have risen again during the night. You must follow up her tracks, even though it is to fall in with her father. *Ah, ma chèrie! ma pauvre enfant!* it is some harm will come to you! But I will myself go——"

"Steady, Jeannette!" said the sergeant. "I will go." For at that moment the fear that had been troubling him one half the night took shape and rose up before him. And that was, if the girl kept on travelling expecting to meet her father but did not, and were she unable to return : or a little wind sprung up that would obliterate her tracks and prevent them following her, she must inevitably perish. The thought chilled his heart.

Just then there came a furious pounding at the door, and a voice that there was no mistaking cried—

"Hilloa there, Yorke! Darn you, Yorke! What the dickens is the matter with the women?"

The sergeant went to the door and opened it.

"Nothing, sir," he answered, "only one of them has gone during the night—Mademoiselle St. Denis."

"What! and us watching the door! Well, of all

the artful young——" But for once in his experience
Jamie's vocabulary of opprobrious terms failed to
furnish him with a word vile enough to suit him.
He mumbled strangely. Then surprise and mortification silenced him. But, in an unguarded moment,
he pushed past the sergeant, and made for Marie's
bedroom. At the same moment Dick Townley and
the scout, alarmed by the outcry Jamie had raised,
entered the kitchen to find out what all the trouble
was about.

Unfortunately for the officer, he had forgotten the
warning he had received on two former occasions
regarding the entering of the kitchen. And now,
before Jeannette had almost time to recover from
her astonishment, the commissioned cad had entered
the bedroom of the girl, had begun to pull about the
bedclothes, to throw them on the floor, and to get
down on his knees, and peer under the bed.

With a cry and a spring, like that of a wounded
animal, the half-breed woman made for the stove ;
snatched from it a burning fagot of wood ; with her
spare hand seized the iron dipper full of hot water—
which indeed had never been off the stove—and
darted into Marie's room after the officer. The
sergeant endeavoured to stop her by getting between her and the officer ; but she thrust the
burning fagot into his face till it singed his mous-
tache and eyelashes.

" *Tenez-vous là !* Back, you !" she cried, and the

gleaming of her black eyes betrayed her Primitive
fiery origin ; " back, as you value your life ! I
should be sorry to hurt you whom I have no quarrel
with."

And now that ignoble day of reckoning, which all
blasphemers and bullies bring upon themselves, came
to Jamie; and it came at the hands of the sex for
which he had so little respect.

Jeannette surprised the officer in the little room.

" *Parbleu !* " she hissed between her teeth.
" *Coquin !* You blackguard, low man—you would
dare enter the room of my dear mistress, would
you ? "

" Stand back, woman ! Stand back, you demned
tiger-cat ! Do you know who I am ? " cried Jamie,
the thought of the exalted position which political
influence had won for him suggesting itself to him.
" I am an officer—— "

Swish ! went the scalding water over his coarse,
cowardly face ; but he partly saved himself by
throwing up his hands. In a second he had
caught up some bedclothes so as to throw them
over her. But she was too quick for him, and down
came the burning billet of wood upon his broad
shoulders. The sergeant, alarmed for the safety of
his superior, essayed another rush in upon her. But
he received a sharp rap on the head—just meant as
a gentle hint to him to mind his own business—that
caused him to stagger out of the room again. Dick

Townley and the scout merely looked on. They would hardly have moved one finger to save their officer from his well-merited disgrace, even though ordered to. It was an illustration upon a small scale of the truth conveyed in these verses of Tennyson's beginning with—

"He who rules by terror, doeth grievous wrong."

It is safe to say that if Dick Townley felt ashamed of the cloth he wore just then, he, otherwise, enjoyed himself.

Then the officer clutched at, and succeeded in wrenching the billet of wood from Jeannette's hand. But she pounced on him like the tigress that she was ; tore his hair, and scratched him after the most approved style of Chinamen and women in general. She was a strong woman ; she cuffed and buffeted him, knocked his head against the wall, and when at last the sergeant and the other two men thought it fit to interfere, and pull her off her prey, a more sorry and wretched-looking specimen of humanity than Jamie could not well be imagined. As the three men held her, the officer, with a look of mingled terror and rage on his face, seized the smouldering billet of wood, and advanced upon her as if to strike her with it.

"Down with that billet of wood!" thundered the sergeant. "Damn it, would you strike a woman who is being held ?"

Jamie started back transfixed with astonishment. Such unparalleled insolence and rank insubordination he had never met with before. But he stayed his hand. That look in the sergeant's eye was ominously like the light that glowed in that mad half-breed woman's. He only stammered—

" You heard that, Townley? You heard what the sergeant said ? "

" Heard what ? " said the private ; " I heard him remind you, in the most humble and civil manner, that you were an officer of the North-West Mounted Police, and that it was a woman you wanted to strike with a billet of wood, when she was being held. Oh, I'll swear to that ! "

The officer groaned.

" Pierre," he cried, in a frenzied way, "you heard the sergeant damn me ; didn't you ? "

" I heard you damn the sergeant," answered the scout, testily ; "and I saw you kick a woman. I think it would be your wisest plan your tongue to hold ! "

" Oh, Je—rusalem ! " cried the officer.

" I would beg of you, sir, to leave the room," said the sergeant. " You see, we can't hold the woman here all day ; and I suppose you will want to start off after the girl."

The sorely discomfited officer thought—as best he could—that it was the better thing to do under the circumstances, and left the room. He was also some

what apprehensive lest Jeannette should break loose
again, and be after him ; and this was a contingency
to be guarded against. No sooner had the officer left
than Harry Yorke placed the now perfectly passive
woman gently in a chair. A reaction had set in, and
her demeanour underwent a complete change. She
was now indulging in a hearty cry. " Oh, to think
that I should have lowered myself like that," she
sobbed. " But to hear that villain talk of my young
mistress as he did——," and here she could not find
words to express her indignation.

" You have made him pay for it, Jeannette," said
Yorke. " And, by Jove ! I suppose it's rank treason
for me to say so, but, as my superior officer, I'm
heartily ashamed of him. Thank goodness I've only
a couple of months more to put in now ; for I could
not stand much more of this sort of thing."

In the meantime the scout had gone out and
fetched a supply of firewood in for Jeannette; then
he lifted away the box of ashes for her from her
stove. The trooper took the water buckets and,
taking them to the well, filled them. As for
Jeannette, she was a kind-hearted if impulsive soul,
and these simple little actions touched her. She
was now heartily ashamed of her late outbreak,
being usually the best tempered of women—though
like the best tempered, the most dangerous when
roused—but still she kept lamenting about Marie.
So in order to facilitate matters, and hurry them

out to follow up the tracks of her young mistress, she herself prepared breakfast for them while they were saddling up. After a somewhat hurried meal, they were in the saddle once more. Jamie, by this time, had somewhat recovered his equanimity: he thought that by following up the tracks of the girl he would come upon her father, and make an easy capture; this raised his spirits. As he had little sense of shame, the light in which he had so lately figured soon ceased to trouble him. The marks of Jeannette's finger nails, and the place where the billet of wood had struck him, however, kept on troubling. They promised to keep the incident green in his memory for some little time. But he was one of those men whom it is difficult to insult, an absence of self-respect rendering such a contingency almost an impossibility. He had, however, sufficient sense to see that he had not figured in a particularly creditable light, and that the private and the scout would back up the non-com. in a matter of evidence. He therefore determined to bide his time and " land all three," as he felicitously put it to himself, in some other way.

"Get on her trail, Pierre," cried the officer; " surely, you can track a human being in the snow."

But either the little scout was unaccountably stupid that morning, or else the girl had shown considerable skill in avoiding the wreaths of snow, for he wasted some considerable time before he picked up her tracks. Indeed, it was not until after he had a whispered colloquy with the sergeant that he did so. No very great quantity of snow had indeed fallen : it was the way it had drifted before the wind that had given the impression of quantity. However, it was not so easy to follow up her tracks as they thought it would have been ; for the girl, as has been said, seemed to have chosen the deepest and most treacherous drifts to walk upon, only stepping on these long strips that the wind had laid bare on purpose to give them some difficulty in picking her tracks up again. She had crossed and recrossed the rugged and tortuous creek in a most exasperating fashion. The result was that in places which she had passed over on snow-shoes leaving but little visible impression, their horses sank and floundered about in a dangerous manner. On more than one occasion, the officer, chafing under the delay, and eager to show the scout that he was not going fast enough, would put spurs to his horse and shoot ahead for fifty yards or so. Then, all at once, he would disappear in a drift or into the concealed bed of the creek, where nothing would be seen of him save his bear-skin cap, and the fine snow-dust flying into the air as his poor horse plunged and pawed helplessly. However, Jamie could always be heard. Yuba Bill, or a Queensland bullock driver could not have expressed himself more forcibly on such occasions. The delay thus occasioned by extricating him from such positions was considerable. On one occasion the scout, whose plan it was to throw his lariat over the officer's head and shoulders, and thus draw him out, pulled "rather prematurely," as Dick Townley characterised it, and the rope tightening round Jamie's neck nearly succeeded in strangling him before they realised his position.

But all this time Harry Yorke was sorely disturbed in his own mind. He knew that if by now the girl had not met her father, she must be exhausted, and unable to proceed farther. If she had met her father, say three or four hours before that time, then, her father and his partner having time enough, could either hurry past them by some other route up the coullees which they knew so well, or else they could throw off the liquor. And if they were taken empty handed, then the police had no hold upon them. But if she had not met her father, and had sunk down exhausted on that shelterless prairie, might not she have given way to that insidious death-sleep, and be even now beyond the reach of earthly succour? The thought struck through him like a knife. They must hurry on at any hazards—it was getting on for mid-day now. His mind was made up, he must speak to the officer.

"I beg your pardon, sir," he said ; "how would it do to make for that bend of the creek we see about three miles off, and cut the tracks. You see, she must have followed down this creek. It's little use losing time, and playing out our horses following it round. Besides, I am not quite sure if we can do that anyhow. It's an awkward place—'Dead-man's Gully,' we call it, where some Indians are buried. I am sure it will be all but impassable just now."

"Why the dickens didn't you suggest that before?" was the officer's somewhat unreasonable reply, seeing that the proposed short cut had only just presented itself. Then he added querulously, "Blow me, but it seems I've got to do the thinking for the whole party. I don't know what on earth would become of you fellows if you hadn't a man with a head on him to do the thinking part of the business for you."

It was just on the tip of Dick Townley's tongue to utter a pious "Amen" in a spirit of mild sarcasm, but he luckily recollected himself just in time, and preserved a discreet and proper silence. As for the sergeant, he bore the attempted snub as he bore many others, with a spirit of patient submission, albeit he could safely have told the officer that he—the inspector—being in charge of the party, was supposed to do the thinking.

If Jamie and his worthy compeer, M'Turk (the enlightened individual who said "a horse's life was of more importance than a man's," and that "a policeman was a machine and not supposed to think"), had been a couple of mules hitched up together in a team,

one of them would have backed over a precipice for
the sheer satisfaction of pulling the other with it and
having its own way.

It was noon now, and they had again cut the tracks
of the girl as they approached the creek. They were
making for a little ridge about half a mile ahead of
them, which would command a comprehensive view
of the prairie and the gateway of the Devil's Playground, when the scout, who had been riding in
advance, suddenly checked his horse, and gave a low
whistle. The others " loped " up. In the snow, and
travelling from the south-east to north-west, was a
waggon track.

"Done!" gasped Jamie, growing purple in the face;
"she's met them, and has given us the slip, and
they've made for Medicine Hat. Oh! by the beard
of Julius Cæsar, some of you fellows 'll languish in
Joey Trigot's hotel yet for this."

He spoke frantically, and, it must be confessed,
somewhat confusedly. His remarks regarding the
hotel had reference to those historic quarters under
the tender charge of the provost-sergeant, dignified
by the name of the guard-room, where members of
the rank and file too frequently enjoyed terms of
enforced hospitality for slight breaches of discipline.
Honoured rank and file: Louis Riel, Gaudier,
Racette, and other murderers in these same cells have
partaken of a like hospitality, and cheered you with
their playful remarks as, separated by a half-inch

board, you rose in the morning to the exhilarating strains of *reveille*.

The sergeant, as if he had not heard the officer's remarks, spoke.

"But where is the girl? You see her tracks go right on to the ridge. She must be somewhere on the prairie, for this waggon has crossed her tracks. She must have gone on long before this waggon came up, and whoever was in the waggon cannot have noticed her tracks. The girl must perish if some one does not follow her up!"

"Let her——"

But he did not finish his sentence; the look upon the face of the non-commissioned officer terrified him. Bully that he was, he literally quailed before the "What!" that thundered from the lips of the sergeant. But he recovered himself, and cried—

"You, Pierre, get on this waggon track and follow it up; and you, Yorke and Townley, go with Pierre. Look here, I give you a written order," and, cold as it was, he took a note-book and pencil from his buffalo-coat pocket, and, scrawling something on it, threw it to the sergeant. "That'll protect you," he said. "I guess I'm running this show, and not you. I'll answer to Larry."

This was Jamie's habitual way of talking of the Commissioner, so it was not to be wondered at if there was sometimes considerable disregard paid to

relative rank amongst a certain class in the North-
West Mounted Police Force.

"Then, sir, will you see after the girl?" asked the
sergeant, respectfully. "You see, if she perishes,
there will be an inquiry, and, of course—I mean no
disrespect—the circumstances of the case will all come
out."

"Go on, oh, go on!" roared Jamie. "None of
your cockneyfied insolence! I'll stop here in the
meantime—that's more than enough for you. You'd
better get a rustle on, and catch up with old St.
Denis, for it's him, beyond doubt."

Jamie chuckled to himself as he watched the party
out of sight. Then he drew a pipe from his pocket,
already charged, and began to smoke. Soon he got
off his horse and sat on the snow. But before long
the intense frost froze up his pipe, and he had to stop
smoking. How long he would have sat in that
enviable, trance-like state peculiar to him it is need-
less to speculate upon, but the coldness of his seat
forced itself upon him in a rather disagreeable
manner. He then led his horse by the bridle rein
and endeavoured to follow Marie St. Denis' tracks,
but he got into a drift and floundered about helplessly. (The irreverent private had said that Jamie
in a snowdrift resembled a porpoise in a barrel of
sawdust.) On the still air of that prairie there arose
a choice flow of language that had even the badgers
happened to be out and overheard would have

shocked their notions of propriety. At last he got clear of the drift.

" No use," he said to himself. " Can't follow the wench up, though I would have liked to. Strikes me the best thing I can do is to follow Yorke, and capture the waggon. Guess there will be lots of good stuff on board, and a nip wouldn't go bad this morning."

And no sooner had he come to this conclusion than he jumped on his horse, and, putting spurs to it, loped after the waggon, which had evidently been driven by one who had a thorough knowledge of the snow-clad prairie, for the tracks meandered along the clear, wind-swept ridges, where travelling was comparatively easy ; and, while pursuing a certain course, always avoided snowdrifts and treacherous spots on either side.

CHAPTER XII.

A PURSUIT, A CAPTURE, AND A SURPRISE.

IT was now well on in the afternoon, and the sun shone clearly out, as he always does in the North-West no matter how low the thermometer is. Though there was no warmth in his rays, still they gave a feeling of life even to that ghastly, featureless landscape. The snow glowed and shimmered like burnished silver; millions of diamond-like crystals scintillated and sparkled in a dazzling fashion on its surface. It is this painful glittering of the sun's rays upon the snow that causes snow-blindness, which many dwellers in these regions know to their cost.

For some hours the police party had been following up the tracks of the waggon, but as yet had been unable to overtake it.

"*Mon Dieu!*" exclaimed the little scout at length, "how they must have travelled! But overtake them we shall yet! For the Medicine Hat Ranche they will make, and, surely, their horses cannot travel farther—ours won't, anyhow. But here comes *Monsieur* the Inspector."

The sergeant stopped fearfully and looked round.
It was as the scout had said ; it was his superior
officer—and alone. Harry Yorke experienced a
strange sinking at his heart—where was the girl ?
And there rose up before him a vision of Marie St.
Denis upon some ridge of that lonely prairie, looking
around wistfully for the succour that came not, and
striving bravely but vainly to resist the spells of
the king of dreams whose realms border on that
land from which no wanderer may retrace his steps.

"Did you not find her, sir?" the sergeant asked
the inspector with a tremor in his voice that struck
the officer as not a little ominous.

"No; I tried to follow up the tracks, but the
snow got so confoundedly deep that I couldn't.
How is it you have not overhauled the waggon by
this time?"

Harry Yorke regarded his superior almost stupidly
for a few seconds. The gravity of the situation and
the sense of his own helplessness crushed down upon
him with a sickening force. Then a fit of anger and
rebellion at his superior's palpable inhumanity seized
him. In another moment he would certainly have
forgotten himself—have said or done something that
would have given his superior officer his much desired
hold upon him, had not the private pressed quietly
towards him, and, with a look of deep concern on his
face, whispered something to him.

"Let's hope that it may be as you say, Dick," he

said, in answer, " and there's just a chance that it may be so. As you say, she is a strong girl and a sensible one, and would not be likely to risk walking farther south than she could walk back again by daylight. But I know what walking in this rare atmosphere means ; one keeps on walking till one discovers all at once that the limbs are played out and it is impossible to go a foot farther."

" Look here, Harry," said his friend, " we cannot be very far behind this waggon now. Let us hurry up and overtake it—we may learn something. I've a presentiment that everything is all right. If not, we can go back and find out where the girl is, let Jamie call it what he likes, rank insubordination or desertion, I'll go with you. We cannot be more than a few miles from the ranche now at the outside."

The private's advice, under the circumstances, was the most sensible course to take just then ; the party pushed on again over wind-swept ridges and frozen sloughs. The travelling was comparatively easy, for the person who had driven the waggon must have had a thorough knowledge of the prairie to have chosen a route that was so free from any obstructions.

To be upon the unbroken, treeless prairie in winter-time is for all the world like being at sea with the sun shining on the water. There is the blurred and seemingly boundless horizon, and there are the wave-like heights and hollows in the nearer foreground, the former foam-crested and wonderfully

natural. It is as realistic as any wintry northern
sea on which the sun has deigned to smile for a brief
space.

Now they loped along a frozen and tufted rib of
land, and then they ploughed their way through a
slough where the long grass had caught and held the
drifting snow. It was a clear, cold day. At one
time in the heavens they saw that remarkable pheno-
menon which is said to herald a spell of unusually
hard weather, the mock sun with a number of rings
of light intersecting one another, large and brilliant,
and multiplied with kaleidoscopic effect.

And now the country became more broken; they
were descending the side of a coullee, when the little
scout cried out and pointed to a dark speck, which,
on closer observation, turned out to be a waggon far
out on the plain.

"That's it! that's it!" cried Jamie, excitedly.
"We've got him now! I hope it's decent whiskey,
for I can do a drop, I can tell you."

"What on earth are you doing?" cried the
sergeant, aghast; for the officer had made the
private hand over his carbine to him, had dismounted,
and was fixing the sight.

"Why, going to stop that there waggon to be
sure," answered Jamie.

Before the sergeant could stop him, he had knelt
down on the snow and taken aim—*ping*, there was
a roar that grew and died away again in that

unfettered expanse. Suddenly a beautiful conical jet of snow spurted into the air between them and the waggon. It was like a whale spouting at sea, or a cannon-ball striking the water and just skimming the surface.

The sergeant heaved a sigh of relief.

"I would not fire again if I were you, sir," said the latter, in vain trying to conceal his indignation at the summary and incriminating measures which his superior officer was adopting. "That sort of thing might have been legal enough a few years ago, but the country has decreed that a Mounted Policeman has no more right to murder a man in cold blood than any other body. What if you had killed the man in the waggon?"

Jamie, who had just been going to dilate upon the splendid direction of the shot he had just fired, tried to pass the matter off with a miserable and uneasy laugh. To tell the truth, the shot surprised no one so much as Jamie himself; for it happened to be a standing joke with the men that Jamie could not hit a hay-stack at twenty yards.

But the waggon did not stop, it only quickened its pace, and the horses were seen to be stretching out over the level prairie. In another mile or so the ranche would be reached ; there it would be easy to throw off a number of small kegs of liquor where the police could not find them. The sergeant pressed his heels into his horse's sides and started off at a

canter. Just then the officer's horse stumbled into
a badger-hole; in another second Jamie had dismounted abruptly and in an unregimental fashion.
The private and the scout pulled up to assist him.

The sergeant was close upon the waggon. He
could see some one in it reclining on what seemed
to be a bale of robes, but which he reckoned were
kegs of whiskey. The person, whoever it was, did
not once turn round to look at him. Another
hundred yards and the ranche would be reached.
It was hardly worth while calling out to the party
in the waggon to stop, for it was already slowing.
In another minute it had turned the corner of a long
straw-shed and pulled up. And now the sergeant,
tired, and not a little annoyed, jumped off his horse
and went forward to the waggon-box. Was it
Gabriel, or François, the former's partner? The
figure, like all figures in the North-West in winter-
time when travelling on the prairie, was heavily
muffled up.

"Now, then," cried the sergeant, testily, "you have
given us a nice chase, haven't you? Don't you think
it would have been just as well for you if you had
stopped when you saw we must inevitably overtake
you?"

The figure turned round and looked full upon him,
and there was something that was almost conscience-
stricken in that look.

Harry Yorke started back as if he had been con-

fronted with a ghost. It was neither Gabriel nor
François his partner. It was Marie St. Denis herself!

The sergeant stared for a minute in speechless
astonishment upon her, for he could not understand
how it was she came to be there. Besides, where
did she get the waggon? and where was her father?
Upon the fair face of the girl, the colour of which
was somewhat heightened, there was neither that
irritating look of satisfaction which comes from the
knowledge of having outwitted some one, nor yet
was there any apprehension. She looked for a
moment into his face, then dropped her eyes again,
and said—

"I am afraid you must think very badly of me.
It would be untrue if I confessed myself sorry for
what I have done, for I am not, although I regret
the necessity that forced me to do it. But I feel that
I have treated you very badly, and made you a very
poor return for your goodness. I did not mean to
deceive you—personally."

"Don't look at it in that light," he said, simply.
"But where is your father?" It was his curiosity,
and not his professional zeal that spoke now.

"Safe," she cried, as a glad light sprang into her
eyes, "and done with the cursed trade for ever. I
shall tell you all about it another time. But, oh! I
am so cold and stiff."

She tried to rise to her feet, but her cramped limbs
refused to act, and she sank down again helplessly.

"I am afraid I am somewhat in the same condition as the poor horses," she said, with rather a pitiable smile; "what you might call 'played out.' Will you relent so far as to help me down?" and her face grew rather white and weary looking, though she tried to appear as if tired Nature were not pressing her hard just then.

To spring up into the waggon and gently catch hold of her was the work of a minute. "Stop that cruel talk about relenting," he said, "you have over-tasked your strength and are numbed with the long drive. But, thank goodness, you are safe; I thought you had been left behind upon the prairie; even now I can hardly make out how you come to be here. It is a very mysterious business indeed. But, anyhow, you are more or less a mystery to me. I wish you were not."

If he had happened to watch her face closely just then he would have seen that a startled, conscious expression came into it for a moment, and that she looked quickly away as if she were fearful of him seeing it.

He placed her in a leaning position against the side of the waggon, and jumped to the ground again. Then he reached over and placed his arms round her. She lay in them as passively as a child might have done as he lifted her out and carried her towards what was evidently the dwelling house; but before they reached it the door opened and a man and a woman came out. They looked for a moment upon Harry Yorke carrying his precious burden with not a little amazement; then the sergeant spoke.

"I have brought you a visitor, Mrs. Petersen, but I am afraid she is rather fatigued. She is my prisoner, and you must see that she does not escape."

Looking at her face just then one would have thought that she took her position as a captive very easily indeed, and that she seemed quite satisfied to remain his prisoner.

"Marie St. Denis, by all that's wonderful!" cried the stout, good-natured looking woman. "Well, well, now; and just to think of the number of times I have told your father to fetch you along with him when he came; and to think that when you did come it should be in charge of a Mounted Policeman! But I reckon, now that we've got you, we'll keep you for some time. And you, Mr. Yorke! Well, come right in, and you can tell us all about it again. Bless my soul, this is a surprise!"

The sergeant followed the good lady, who talked all the way, into the large and comfortable sitting-room, put Marie St. Denis on a large couch that was wheeled up some little distance from the stove, and went out again to see after the horses. Just then the officer, leading his lame horse, the private and the scout came up. The inspector, in spite of his recent accident, seemed elated at having captured the team.

"Well, who is it?" he asked. "St. Denis, or François, or both?"

"Neither," answered the sergeant, grimly, and with not a little secret pleasure; "only Mademoiselle St. Denis." And he watched the effect of the shot.

"Eh? what—what's that you're saying?" cried Jamie, staring at him with wide-open eyes and as if he had not heard aright.

"Well, go in and look for yourself," answered the sergeant, forgetting himself, and remembering how the girl might have perished only some few hours before through the officer's inhumanity. "If you had followed up her tracks," he continued, "we might have been saved this wild-goose chase."

He did not say how glad he was that they did not follow up her tracks.

"But surely," cried Jamie, with a look of ludicrous fear and incredulity on his face as he rushed to the waggon and clambered into it, "surely, they haven't sold us? Where is the whiskey? Why, the waggon's empty! Sold, by——!"

"That's so," interrupted the sergeant, coolly, watching the officer as he turned over the buffalo robes and searched amongst the loose hay at the bottom of the waggon. "You see, it's this way: there must have been *two* waggons. The girl met them early this morning and told them about us. They loaded all the stuff upon one waggon and sent it on in another direction; then she must have got into the empty one and, making a circle, cut her old tracks, knowing that we should follow up the first track we came to, like the geese we were. She judged rightly. The other waggon may be at Maple Creek or Walsh by this time and have unloaded. It is getting dark now and, anyhow, they're safe enough. I am afraid, sir, this day's work will make a very unsatisfactory report—'captured one girl and an empty waggon.'"

The sergeant seemed to take a malicious pleasure in laying the facts of the case ruthlessly before his superior officer.

"Hold your tongue! Oh, hold your blanked English tongue!" cried Jamie, frantically, and somewhat inconsistently. Then for a few minutes he plunged around aimlessly, beside himself with rage.

As for Dick Townley and the little scout, they were evidently in no way dissatisfied with the turn things had taken. Even the sorry state of mind their superior officer was in seemed in no way to damp their spirits. Indeed, quite the reverse.

"Let me see that wench," cried Jamie, angrily, as if seized with a sudden thought. "I'll teach her to fool the police this way."

He strode towards the house. But the rancher stood between him and it.

"Mr. Inspector," he said, quietly and deliberately, "you don't enter my house : these three gentlemen are

welcome to ; I only allow gentlemen into it. I am,
and have always been, friendly towards the police,
and regret this little affair, because I have been on
terms of intimacy with many of your brother officers
who are gentlemen. But I know you; the force
knows you to its cost and disgrace; moreover, the
inhabitants and tax-payers of Canada are getting
tired of supporting such bungling good-for-nothings
as you, who are neither for use nor ornament, and
who at the most only represent a few votes down
east. Recollect, you wear the Queen's uniform : as a
loyal subject I ought not to lay a finger on you ; but
try and make your way into this house and I'll kick
you out. I will—so help me——. There is the men's
shack over there ; you can go into it—it is any
amount good enough for you."

As for the representatives of the rank and file
present, it is quite possible that they felt the painful
nature of this speech much more keenly than the
officer did. But this is only what might have been
expected.

As for the little scout, he hummed audibly to
himself, " *Victoria, Victoria, witty witty wit pom,
pom,*" and felt as if he stood at least six inches taller
in his mocassins.

But here it is necessary to explain more fully
how Marie St. Denis came to be driving the empty
waggon ; and how she assisted her father and his
partner to evade the police.

On that same morning, when she had struggled to the wind-swept ridge, gazed apprehensively around, and could see no signs of her father coming : when her overtaxed energies gave way, and the over-powering desire to sleep overcame her, it was perilously near being her last hour on earth. Indeed, the attendant signs and tokens that are vouchsafed by the King of Terrors to his victims, were fast being made manifest to her. " As we live, we die," is a saying as old as the hills, and as true as the develop-ment of all things from primary elements : willed and inaugurated by that Omniscient and Divine Being who has given man dominion over the earth, and made him a responsible̤ servant under Him—a servant, but a lord of Creation in his own right. It has been shown how the girl looked towards the portals of that mysterious valley, the Devil's Play-ground, and how she could see no signs of help coming from them. But there was help there if she only could have known of it. In the lee of a semi-circular wall of fantastically coloured clay, surrounded by a scraggy growth of willows, and within fifty yards of the entrance, a couple of teams were camped. Grouped together in another sheltered spot a little farther up eight or nine horses were standing round the last of some baled hay, and seemed in no way inconvenienced by the coldness of the weather ; the broncho-bred equine of the North-West, with his shaggy coat and sturdy constitution, will " rustle " for

himself and grow fat in the winter-time when eastern-
bred horses will perish.   There was a tent close to one
of the waggons, and two men in it had just finished
breakfast.   There was a tiny portable stove in the
tent, and a small pile of wood handy.

"Well, François," said one who was no other than
Gabriel St. Denis, "it's as well we made this place
before the blizzard kem up ; but as it is, no perticlar
depth of snow has fallen.   I guess I'll just go out and
tek a leetle look round.   Then we kin hitch up and
travel up Wild Horse coullee—I could find my way
blindfolded thar."

" *Très bien*," said François.   " Put the saddle on
Jacques then, and choose a road out of these *mau-
vaises terres pour traverser*.   In the meantime I will
the decks clear, and the horses hitch up until you
come.   I will leave the tent till last thing."

In a few minutes more Gabriel was on the back
of Jacques and was standing on the elevated ground,
just outside the portals of the mysterious valley.
The latter, indeed, was a good place to have taken
shelter in : a regiment of soldiers might have passed
within a stone's throw of them and missed them.
Keenly Gabriel scanned the ghastly stretch of snow-
clad prairie.   Suddenly he started.   What was that
black object on the crest of that lonely ridge ?   What
was the meaning of that dark speck hovering in mid-
air on balanced pinion just above it ?   And what was
the meaning of that slinking, furtive, feline-like brute

that approached the thing on the ground with malignant tread, and by an ever narrowing circuitous route: every now and again stopping to raise its fanged and wicked-looking snout, to prick its wolf's ears as it looked around, to sniff the air, and see that the coast was clear?

"For where the carcase is——" said Gabriel to himself.

It was a remarkable presentiment that took possession of him just then. But, whichever way it was, the terrible thought no sooner flashed upon him than he dug his heels into his horse's ribs and darted towards that dark object.

"God help me if it is so!" he cried aloud.

And perhaps it was the few minutes of apprehensive agony which followed, that made him so amenable to the dictates of conscience and the voice of his daughter afterwards.

It was indeed Marie who had sunk into that slumber from which she might never have awakened. He was just in time, and, flinging himself from his horse, he pulled off her mitts; but her hands had not been frozen, so he chafed them between his own. It seemed almost a pity to awaken the girl; there was such a look of contentment on her face. Then he called on her by name, and she opened her eyes. It was a strange thing that she seemed in no way surprised to see him there; she merely said, "Then I did not dream I saw you coming from the Devil's

Playground, father; I have heard and seen such
strange things."

"Thank God!" said Gabriel to himself piously—
smuggler and all that he was. He had a shrewd,
uncomfortable guess what brought her there.

"But you must not lie here, Marie. You must
come over to the tent and have some hot tea. Can
you stand?"

He raised her to her feet; but she would have
fallen had he not placed his arm round her. He
caught her up, and placing her upon the back of his
horse, took her as quickly as he could over to the
camp.

The bird of prey, that had been wheeling round her
head in ever narrowing circles, hovered undecidedly
around for a minute or two, then shot off in disgust
to look somewhere else for his breakfast. The wolf
ascended the little ridge and sniffed around the spot
where the girl had lain, then, partly raising his head,
gazed after them with relaxed, drooping jaws and
sullen, wondering eyes. Then he raised his head still
higher and yawned horribly, till one could have seen
the bluish ribbed roof of his mouth, and counted
every gleaming yellow tooth in his head. One would
have shuddered to see the almost human expression
of baffled cunning and design that the face of the
brute suggested. He, also, would have to look somewhere else for his breakfast.

Once in the warm tent and refreshed by some hot

tea (there is no stimulant so safe and lasting in its effects after exposure as tea) and something to eat, Marie felt little the worse of her journey. But before she had taken anything she had set their line of action before them. She had told them, as they had guessed, what brought her there.

"You must either go back to the States, father, with the cargo, or else go on to the ranche, alone and empty-handed. But whatever you do, this business must cease here, now and for ever," she said, determinedly.

"You're talking nonsense, child," said Gabriel. "We kennot recross the Milk River Ridge now. Besides, the cargo's worth over two thousand dollars, and we ken't afford to throw it away. We must scheme so's to pass through somehow."

"Do you think, father," said the girl, indignantly, and showing, as honest François, Gabriel's partner, noted, that there was a strong suggestion of a chip of the old block in her, "do you think for a moment that I begged the help of one, before whom I had to sacrifice my pride, for the sake of enabling you to still further carry out your schemes? No! ten thousand times *No!*"—she stamped her foot as if she were commanding a subject, and looked her father steadily in the eyes—" I came to save you from yourself, father. I did not come to help you to cheat the police. You must do as I bid you, and quit this place for good. You may excuse yourself as you may, but you are

committing an injustice on me. Would you have
done this had my mother been alive ? "

She had never spoken like this in her life before to
her father, and he stared at her wonderingly. There
was one who had died when Marie was a mere child
—whom he had often seen live again in the girl's
eyes, and now he saw the mother live and speak in
the person of the woman ; trembling, he passed
one hand before his eyes so that he might shut out
the sight. But her voice still rang in his ears, and he
felt like one who is detected in a crime. Perhaps
Gabriel had never realised the error of his ways as he
did then. As for François, who was a bachelor and a
good-hearted man, though he secretly admired her
spirit he could not comprehend her scruples. But
women to François were mysterious and inexplicable
creatures at the best, and he had long since given up
trying to understand them. Though he thought, in
his simple, honest way, that there was nothing so
particularly dreadful in being tyrannised over by
such a girl as this particular one before him, still
he felt thankful to Providence that he was yet a
bachelor, and free from the annoyances of petticoat
government.

"But," argued Gabriel, weakly and irrelevantly,
" it won't do to leave the whiskey here. S'posin' the
pleece git it, we're goners both. We ken't cache it ;
fur in this snow they'd spot it only too quick. We
must git a rustle on, an' git through with it. François
ken't go on hisself——"

" *Tenez-vous là !* " interrupted François, " I kin."

" Now, listen," said Marie, " there is only one thing you can do. Put all the wretched stuff on one waggon—if half of it did not belong to you, François, I'd make father spill it—and you, François, take it anywhere out of the way. You, father, had better go back, and on foot, to the ranche ; for to-morrow the police will make back and find you there. If you are found without contraband goods they cannot interfere with you. I shall take the empty waggon in two hours' time from now, and going back cut my own tracks. The police will at once follow up the waggon tracks, and I will make straight for the Medicine Hat Ranche ; knowing every foot of the way it need not take long ; but it will take so long that they will not be able to go farther to-day. By to-morrow you ought not to care who finds you."

" Good girl," said François, in admiration. " *Mon Dieu*, what a smuggler you would have made ! "

Poor François, it was the only compliment he could think of just then ; men are such stupid creatures sometimes. However, this proposition just suited him ; he could push on up Willow Creek, and round by the head of the mountain, now that he knew where the police were, without any fear of inter-ruption, and with four good horses he could make Walsh sometime that night. He knew every foot of the ground. As for Gabriel, he could do without him ; it were better that he should go home, and

when the police found him there it would be better
for both of them.   They would not know what to
make of the affair.   The girl was a good, brave girl,
and what she had done, and what she offered to do,
was what ninety-nine girls out of a hundred would
neither have thought of, nor yet attempted.   François
loyally seconded her proposition.

"But, Marie, you ken't go alone : you must let
me go with you," said Gabriel.

"There is no danger," said the girl.   "The police
will not be at any time so very far behind me should
anything go wrong.   Now, go and do as I have told
you ; let me sleep for an hour or so and I shall be
able for my work.   You can have the horses hitched
up and ready for me before you wake me."

And then the girl lay down in the warm tent—for
a tent with even the tiniest stove in it is a very warm
abode in the coldest weather, contrary to what some
might think—and slept a refreshing and safe sleep.
As for the two men they had no time to lose.   They
put the dutiable goods into one of the waggons, and,
hitching up four of the best horses into it, François
started off.   Having hunted the buffalo and the deer
for years in the country he had to travel over, it is,
perhaps, unnecessary to add that by nightfall he had
safely got rid of his cargo alongside the main line of
the Canadian Pacific Railway.

Gabriel watched the girl while she slept, and now
that François had gone, and he was alone with his

own thoughts, he had a bad time with them. He had told himself, over and over again, that all the illegal adventures he had been connected with, that all the money which, somehow, he had lately got so fond of amassing, were all for the sake of Marie, and that she would be benefited in the end. But now —and the thought startled him with a painful implacability—what if this last uncalled-for adventure had cost Marie her life, what then had been his gain ? Would not all the money that he had been striving after for years be so much dross to him, and hateful in his sight? Would his case not be like that of the man who, in gaining the whole world, lost his own soul? He pictured her as he had seen her lying on that ghastly ridge, sleeping that sleep that might know no waking. Surely in his finding her then there was the finger of Providence pointing to a solemn warning. How near, how terribly near, that dread realisation it had been. He could bear the thought no longer, and sprang to his feet. Then he fell on his knees, and in that tent, and in the presence of his sleeping daughter, he grovelled in an agony of shame.

He uttered a few broken and imperfect words ; but they died upon his lips. How could a man like him dare to pray? Was it not like mere blasphemous presumption on his part to thank God for her deliverance? Not that he in his heart had looked upon the traffic he was engaged in as a grievous sin ;

but what right had he, as a father, to risk the life and
happiness of his child ? If he, in his sense of what
was right and what was wrong, feared in his humiliation, to ask God for forgiveness, then, perhaps, there
was some virtue in his abnegation, for he rose from
his knees a better man.

Then Gabriel hitched up the horses into the
waggon, and soon the girl awoke of her own accord.
She drank some hot tea, and partook of some food,
and, as she herself declared, was " fit for any amount
of exposure and fatigue." But she was adamant
when she refused to allow her father to accompany
her.

"You must wrap me well up in the robes, dad,
and make your own way back to the ranche. I know
every foot of mine ; have I not driven on the prairie
scores and scores of times ? "

He wrapped her carefully up as he was bid ; then,
with sad misgivings, he saw her drive off. He
watched as, with skilled hand and practised eyes, she
guided the horses by a circuitous route back to where
she cut her own tracks ; and long after, when horses
and waggon had become a dark wavering speck on
the prairie, he kept gazing after her. He did not
leave that elevated spot he had climbed to until
about an hour and a half afterwards, when he saw
the approach of the police party. When he observed
them get upon her trail and follow it up, he knew
that she was safe, and now he could go on his way.

He slipped on the snowshoes she had left with him, and made a bee-line back to the ranche.

Next day, when the police party made back to Gabriel's place, they met him on his way to bring back the empty waggon that Marie had driven off. But they could not interfere with him. The drifting snow in the night had obliterated all tracks; and, perhaps, they knew it was useless asking him questions. Dick Townley avers that he saw the sergeant take Gabriel out on the prairie, and if the latter "ever got a wigging in all his life, he got one then." The youthful trooper also remarked that Gabriel never lifted his head when Harry Yorke was hotly declaiming, but kept it sunk on his breast as if he knew he were getting something that he deserved.

As for Marie, it has already been shown how she led the police a pretty dance. It was a unique thing, truly, for a girl who, only a few hours before, had been perilously near that bourne from which no traveller returns, to be guiding a waggon over the prairie, and indulging in all sorts of speculations. But such are the recuperative powers of youth and sleep that, when one comes to think of the circumstances, there was nothing so very remarkable in it after all. Truly, as the sage said, Woman is a many-minded creature. It would have puzzled the sage still more to have followed the erratic train of thought which Marie St. Denis indulged in during that long drive ; for Marie's was a complex mind. Who

would have thought, for instance, that one minute
after becoming preternaturally grave, as she specu-
lated on what Harry Yorke would think of her when
he discovered what his promise to her had entailed
upon the police party, she should then indulge in
a mind-picture, in which the gallant police officer
figured prominently.   She thought she saw his face
when he made up upon the team, and discovered
that instead of capturing her father and a cargo of
whiskey, he only found a girl and an empty waggon.
She even laughed merrily to herself when she
pictured that face.   But she had to keep the horses
up to their work so as not to spoil the picture by
any premature disclosure.

As has been hinted at before, the girl's ever-chang-
ing face was a reflex of her mind, and it was a
complex one ; for, while her nature was unselfish,
and had a great capacity for good, there was a considerable spark of old Mother Eve in her after all.

CHAPTER XIII.

A COUPLE of Mounted Policemen are standing on the wooden platform of the Canadian Pacific Railway at Medicine Hat, awaiting the arrival of the east-bound train which is to take them to headquarters at Regina, the capital of Assiniboia. One is the sergeant, Harry Yorke, and the other Dick Townley, the private. They are somewhat differently dressed now that they are travelling per rail. They wear bear-skin caps with yellow badges, fur coats— concealing the dragoon's showy scarlet tunic— dark-blue riding breeches with a yellow stripe, and long, brilliantly-polished top-boots; for the weather is hardly cold enough for moccasins. Standing near them is Pierre, the fat, bright-eyed little scout, with a somewhat lugubrious expression on his face, keeping his eye on a bulky and somewhat dilapidated bundle, which contains some spare wearing apparel that he will on no account have put into the freight van— risky and mysterious receptacle in Pierre's eyes—but will insist on lugging about with him, so precious is it in his sight. The two policemen are, if not actually under arrest, yet going to headquarters for safe keeping, until certain charges that are to be brought against them by Inspector Bounder are investigated. The little scout is going down to give evidence, and to be made use of by doing a little horse-breaking at the same time, much against his will.

And now up comes the heavy train, and they get into one of the long, rather over-heated cars, divest themselves of their overcoats, and prepare to make themselves as comfortable as circumstances will permit. The great bell on the engine clangs, and on they go again.

What immense precipitous cut-banks of clay over-hang the frozen bed of the Saskatchewan river. How typical the wooden and painted Mounted Police post looks on the opposite bank, with its tall flag-staff in the centre of the square. Harry Yorke re-garded it somewhat sadly! "Good-bye, Old Fort," he said; "I spent some happy days in you." He knew he would never be in it again—at least in an official capacity.

Then, with a loud shriek, the train left the Saskatchewan valley, and made a dash at the heavy grade that ascends through the rather pretty valley of Ross Creek into the open prairie a mile or two farther on. In twenty minutes they were out again upon that apparently unbroken and boundless expanse of ocean-like prairie, and bowled along a track which is so level, so straight, and so apparently limitless that to look along it to where the rails become one and meet the horizon line, seems to be looking upon a band of steel that girds the world. Away to the south one could see the broken outline of the Cypress Hills keeping watch over the surrounding country. Sixty miles more, and the little town of Maple Creek is passed, with its stone store—a rather rare thing on these prairies—and two little wooden churches. About a couple of miles to the south, painted white, and just beyond the maple-fringed creek that runs into the prairie, are the Mounted Police barracks. At the station, as at most others, the greater part of the population turned out to witness the great event of the day—the arrival and departure of the cars— and then the train hurried on again. Several miles farther on another station—Colley. But there was nothing at this point save a water-tank and the eternal section-house; not another house in sight; nothing but rolling, snow-clad prairie, and a broken fringe of straggling undergrowth marking the course of the winding creek. Here Harry Yorke looked out somewhat thoughtfully. He could remember when the Governor-General of Canada was travelling through the country, how he had stopped at this point on the previous autumn, and he had made one of the little party who had met the Governor's special train that had been side-tracked, to permit of their enjoying the shooting of some prairie chickens, and a scamper on horseback. Poor Oliver Morphy, his comrade on that occasion ; the dark, cold waters of Lake Winipeg, only a few months before, had claimed a staunch comrade and as leal a heart as ever beat in human breast.

(Light let the turf, under which you were at last laid, rest upon your breast, dear comrade : for your memory is ever with us as green as it in springtime.

In that mysterious land to which we all are journeying, if there be such a thing as a reunion with those who have gone on before, may we meet you there, and feel again the hearty, firm grip of your honest hand. From this side the chasm that yawns between the finite and the eternal, and which death alone can bridge, our hearts go out to you, our all too feeble voices greet you : *Was hiel—Was hiel !*

And you young de Beaujeu, who perished with him : a worthy representative of a worthy race—our loyal fellow subjects the French Canadians. Peace be with you.)

There were quite a few passengers aboard the train, albeit it was the dull season—a few bagmen, one or two disappointed emigrants returning from British Columbia, Seattle or Tacoma, a contingent of naval men from Esquimault, a few Australians who had come by the Yokohama route, a few ranchers from Alberta going east to visit their friends in Lower Canada, and a few belonging to that nondescript genus, the representatives of which are only to be found in perfection on the American Continent. The business of such men lies in cheap and remarkable commodities of a novel and original nature, and in the advertising columns of cheap newspapers : they live by their wits and on the absence of them in other people. Judging by the fact that they always seem to have plenty of money, they must be very wise men indeed, and the people they do business with must be very great fools. The Canadian Pacific Railway somewhat resembles the Suez Canal : it is one of the world's great highways, and a place where, figuratively speaking, all sorts and conditions of strange crafts are congested. The student of human nature has as motley a crowd to study from as he could well find brought together, in a like space, in any part of the world. Moreover, the series of large Pulman cars which permit of the traveller passing from one to the other, and joining any little particular party which he thinks he may safely venture into, makes.what might otherwise be a somewhat long and tedious journey an oft-times entertaining, and by no means unpleasant one.

Despite the rather vague charge of neglect of duty that led to the frustration of the ends of justice, and which the sergeant knew was hanging over him, he did not allow the fact to interfere much with his peace of mind. Indeed, so far as Harry Yorke was concerned, he had a shrewd suspicion that as he had

some time ago not sent in his notice for re-engage-
ment (seeing his term of service expired in about a
month's time), it was just as likely as not that he
should find himself shipped away before then to one
of the farthest outposts of the far North—to Onion
Lake or the Peace River, where he would be entirely
out of touch with the world, and from which (if he
did not re-engage again) it would cost him a small
fortune to get back to the main line of the Canadian
Pacific Railway. This was one of those unpleasant
little mysteries that occasionally crossed the path of
the North-West Mounted Policeman. As to whether
his arch enemy, Inspector Bounder, succeeded or not
in having him reduced to the ranks, was now a matter
of comparatively little moment. He knew that, in
any case, he deserved it. He would not excuse himself in his own eyes ; and though he knew that if he
were placed in a similar position again he would do
exactly as he had done, he realised, all the same, that
no man has a right to allow a selfish love—or call it
what you will—to divert his steps from the straight
path of duty. True, it would gall him in a way that
only one who has striven for and earned his stripes
can feel, to find them rudely taken from him for
" disgraceful conduct," as the powers that be are
pleased to term it with a sublime indifference as to
whether the offence has arisen from an error of judgment or wilful neglect. True, it was considered an
understood and no disgraceful thing in the force for

a man when put upon his trial to make the best even of a bad case; and be it said to the credit of the greater bulk of the officers, they generally gave the arraigned one the benefit of a doubt.

But all these things were of comparative unimportance compared to the one great thought that had gradually grown upon and taken possession of him— what about Marie St. Denis, that girl whose beauty had not only contrasted so strongly with her strange surroundings and gained upon him, but whose innate nobility of mind, and capacity for self-sacrifice, had aroused in him the spirit of admiration, and then the inevitable further development? What was he to do about her? How was he to hear of her? He knew her father had all but completed arrangements to sell out everything, make his way south into the States, and then, with that nomadic spirit of his, and the pride of the girl, it would be a very natural thing indeed for him to lose sight of her altogether. And then——? But would it not be better so—better that he should never see her again? Had he dreamt of such a contingency when he first saw her—of doing such a mad thing as fall in love with her, he would have turned his back on her right there and then. Could he, a man who belonged to a very different sphere of life from that which his present occupation would have denoted, who came of a family of considerable standing, ally himself— assuming, of course, what he had no right to assume,

that the girl herself were willing—to the daughter
of an illiterate adventurer and smuggler whom he
would be ashamed to be seen with in public, even
although the name of the man in question was St.
Denis.

Then he asked himself what his family would say
when they came to hear that he had made, what they
would naturally consider was an undesirable con-
nection? But again, he put the question to himself:
was it not just like the selfish wish of consideration,
peculiar to relatives in general, to want to control his
heart's most sacred promptings, when they would not
move a hand of their own free will to enable him to
earn a crust of bread? True, they had loaded him with
gratuitous advice many a time: sage admonitions
bristling with hoary old saws, when they thought that,
figuratively speaking, it was just possible he meant
" to kick over the traces," when a gentle guiding hand
was all he wanted? Had they not even ignored his
existence altogether, when they feared that a closer
acquaintanceship might mean some slight demand
upon the plethora of their own resources? He was
no cynic or pessimist, although he knew that sweeter
far a crust of bread and independence than the good
things of this life under the uncompromising name of
charity. For in the humbler paths of life that he had
trod, he had met with those who, to the full, realised
the noble truth of that saying, " It is more blessed to
give than to receive." God help the shallow souls

who sneer at the story of the widow's mite! they
want help—badly.

But this were weighing the question from a material
point of view—disposing of it by a selfish and sordid
standard. Yes, even if his family said to him, "you
must not marry one in such and such a station of life ;
you must marry one in ours!" and would not help
him to attain to that position in life which would
enable him to do so. Still, that was no reason to
make him persevere all the more in his obvious
course. Admitting the oft-proved disastrous results
arising from a man being led away by a transient
passion, and marrying one beneath him in moral,
mental, and worldly respects, thus debarring all the
essential welding effects of affinity—was she not, after
all, in most respects his equal ?

He felt, indeed, that in many respects she was infinitely superior to him. So far as her own personality was concerned, she had a face and a manner that
would distinguish her in any sphere of society : there
was little difference between her and any well-born
and cultured Old-Country girl. So far as dress and
certain little unorthodoxies of manner were concerned,
she had a mind that was quick to perceive and
assimilate ; these imperfections—if such they could
be called—were, therefore, not insuperable objections.
Moreover, she was a born gentlewoman although she
had been reared in a log house and her father had
only been a species of adventurer, and smuggler to

boot. Moreover, had she not been partly brought up
in a convent, and received as deep and comprehensive an education as would put the expensive, orna-
mental, and often superficial so-called finished educa-
tions of some of Britain's fashionable ladies' colleges·
to the blush ?   Colleges, where a confused and
meaningless reference to certain art topics, a few glib
references to Herbert Spencer, or the prevailing quasi-
ethical or scientific fad of the day, passes for erudi-
tion.   Besides, she bore the name of St. Denis.   But,
after all, had things been different : had not this cold-
blooded calculating way of weighing all the possible
contingencies militating against his desire to possess
her been satisfactory, it is possible that he would have
been but little influenced by them.   At least he had
come perilously near that stage.   The question that
exercised him most now was—did she care for him ?
Think as he might, she had given him no sign whatever of either positive liking or dislike.   Then his
pride came to his aid, and the thought of a previous
experience to his mind—was he, then, going to stake
his happiness by surrendering himself to the caprice
of any woman ?   He would see if a little delay would
not work a change in him.   The bustle of Regina
would enable him to forget her—if he could.

Then the east-bound train rattled on past Crane
Lake, Gull Lake, Goose Lake, these stretches of
water being now indistinguishable from the leagues
of monotonous rolling prairie by reason of their ice-

THE PULMAN AND THE SNOW-CLAD PRAIRIE. 189

bound and snowy mantles. Every little station-house they passed was exactly like its neighbour. That is, a weather-boarded and gabled two-storied building, painted a warm brown colour, a strip of wooden platform, in front of which were two steel rails which seemed to go out and on into infinite space, and a row of telegraph poles, which dwindled away at the horizon line to a well-defined point, offering one of the finest lessons in perspective that the youthful and inquiring mind could possibly have.

To the unthinking mind, perhaps, this journey over the prairie may be a monotonous one; but to the thinker and the lover of Nature in her many moods, the spirit of grim utilitarianism, in the presence of the engine that hurries him along, is lost sight of; there is, instead, a realisation of that glamour which sur-rounds our youthful conceptions of the illimitable new-world prairie lands—where from the rising to the setting sun the picturesque Red man and the count-less herds of buffalo reigned supreme. It is more than a glimpse of that mystic prairie whose very air is pregnant with romance, and which will stir the blood in the veins of youth, and fire the imagination of old as well as young for all time to come—at least until man has been evolved into that in which all traces of his savage ancestry have been lost, and, therefore, the old instincts cease to move him.

Swift Current, and the welcome intimation " Luncheon is served in the dining-car." And those

of the passengers who could afford 50 cents made for
the second last car—that hotel upon wheels, where,
be it said in justice to the Canadian Pacific Railway, one can always get a substantial and very
daintily served little meal, a good glass of wine, and
a fairly good cigar at a moderate figure.   The C.P.R.
does all things well.

"You and Pierre can go in and have your lunch,"
said Harry Yorke to Townley.   "I don't feel like it
just at present.   I'll come in later on and get a cup
of tea."

"Why, Harry," said the youth, "don't let it——,"
but he broke off suddenly when he looked at his
comrade's face, and only said, " I'm sorry you don't
feel like it, old chap.   If I didn't know you, I'd say
you stood on the dignity of your three stripes.
Allons, Sancho."

And the idea regarding the stripes so seemed to
tickle the irreverent youngster that he indulged in a
grim chuckle.   For the non-commissioned officers of
the Mounted Police, be it said to their credit, relied
in reality more upon the force and influence of their
individuality than any mere supremacy which rank
gave them, which, of course, was essential in its way.
Then the private caught the little scout by the arm,
and marched him along towards the well-appointed
Pulman dining-car.   Here a little incident occurred—
trifling in itself—but serving to show the comedies
we sometimes unwittingly take part in.

CHAPTER XIV.

WHEN Dick Townley and Pierre entered the dining-car they found that they could not get seats together, and so sat down at different tables. Opposite the former, at the same table—each table is seated for four—were two gentlemen, whom he had never seen before. One was a tall, spare, goodly-featured man with a military appearance. He was dressed after a prevailing English fashion, wearing a Norfolk jacket and knicker-breeches. The other was a stout, elderly gentleman who wore a frock-coat, and was unmistakably a Frenchman. By his manner, which was not unkindly, he seemed to be some one of consequence. This conclusion, to a stranger, would have been further fostered by the way the attendants waited upon him. But Private Townley was hungry, and as he considered, properly enough, that a Mounted Policeman, as long as he behaved himself, was just as good as any other body, he sat down opposite the Frenchman of consequence, aforesaid, and politely requested the English-looking gentleman to pass him the bill of fare. This the latter did with a pleasant smile.

The two friends, as they seemed to be, went on talking pleasantly together, apparently oblivious of the private's presence ; and the latter went on with his lunch. Gradually the car somewhat emptied again ; but still the two men opposite Dick Townley sat talking, and he still leisurely continued eating. The English-looking gentleman had ordered a large bottle of claret, and he and his friend were enjoying it. At length the two in the course of their conversation drifted into a controversy as to the pronunciation of the Latin word, *ecce*, as used in the title " *Ecce Homo.*"

" I tell you what,"—Dick did not catch the name— "the pronunciation is *es-ce*. The first 'c' like an 's,' you know," said the English-looking gentleman.

" No, Colonel, I sha'n't have it "—" Americans after all," said Dick to himself—"one ought to pronounce it like *ekky*. 'C' like a 'k,' you know," rejoined the French-looking gentleman, pleasantly.

" Not at all," said the other, " I'm sorry to differ from you ; but—I wonder how we can settle this ? "

He looked hard at Dick, who was modestly draining the last of his pint of Carling, and seemingly satisfied with his scrutiny addressed him quietly.

" Do you—Constable—er——"

" Townley," suggested Dick ; wondering somewhat at this formal but correct mode of address. " At least I understand they christened me so."

" Well, Constable Townley—but pass your claret-glass, I don't think it will disagree with the beer."

He filled up Dick's glass, no dissent being made.

"Might I ask you if you happen to know the proper pronunciation of the word *Ecce*—'*Ecce Homo*,' you know. Is it not pronounced *es-si* ? "

" Sorry to disagree with you," answered Dick, with brutal candour, " but you're wrong."

The smile on his face, however, somewhat made up for the disappointment conveyed in the words.

The English-looking gentleman's face fell somewhat ; the other one laughed loudly, and seemed much elated.

" There, now, Colonel," he cried. " Didn't I tell you you were wrong ! It's *e-k-k-y*. *Ekky Homo*, Mr-er Townley, is it not ? I knew you were wrong, Colonel."

" But you're wrong, too," was the same brutal comment, with the same pleasant smile.

The two gentlemen stared blankly at one another for a minute ; and the one who wore the knicker-breeches said somewhat dryly, but still with a certain significant deference—

" Then how do you pronounce the word ? and, perhaps, you might give us your authority for so

13

doing, at the same time. Surely one of us must be right."

" Doesn't follow," rejoined the youth, easily, but modestly. " There's a third way, if you recognise such a thing as a classical precedent, and that is to pronounce it as if it were *Ex-ce Homo*, the ' c ' like ' x,' you know. Cambridge is my authority." Then he added with a depreciatory little laugh as he held his half-empty claret-glass up to the light, and regarded it with the air of a connoisseur : " But hang it all, you know, gentlemen, I don't see why you should take such a trifling little matter of use-and-wont so seriously. Besides, Cambridge is not immaculate, or the world, after all. It has its little affectations just like other places, for which it can no more give logical reasons than I could if I said the Devil spoke the Irish language and spelt his name with an *h*. You've got institutions in the States that could lay Cambridge long odds in many lines I've no doubt ; at the same time, don't think I mean to disparage Cambridge."

At this stage of the proceedings Dick heard a violent fit of coughing ; looking over the left shoulder of the portly Frenchman, he caught a glimpse of the round moon-like face of Pierre, the scout. On it w a strange look of mingled consternation, entreat and warning. Seeing that he had attracted th private's attention, Pierre straightway indulged i a violent facial pantomime, which, however, failed in its object, in that it only awakened a sense of the ludicrous in the light-hearted private, who could make, so to speak, neither head nor tail of it. That the scout meant to convey some information to him was evident. But, surely, to observe such mystery was absurd. Dick Townley regarded him sternly. He dearly relished a joke at the little scout's expense.

" I say, Pierre," he said loud enough for the scout to hear, and talking over the stout gentleman's shoulder, "what on earth is the matter with you ? you put me in mind of a sick monkey or a nigger with St. Vitus's dance. Can't you behave like a Christian ? Come right forward and talk out like a man if you have anything to say. But, Sancho, old chap, perhaps you'd like to do another bottle of beer first. Just give that little round metal business a dig on the top with your fist ; in polite society the vernacular for this is ' jerking the tinkler,' don't forget that, Pierre."

But Pierre had risen with a look of horror on his face, and, without bestowing another look upon the private, made his way out of the car as quickly as his short legs would carry him.

" Well, I never ! " said Dick Townley, amusedly.

" Nor yet I," echoed the stout gentleman, looking curiously at his companion.

Then, as if something remarkably funny had oc-curred to the three of them, they leant back in their

seats and indulged in a hearty laugh. Just at that
moment, in the mirror that faced the private at the
far end of the car, he saw the door behind him open,
and Harry Yorke, the sergeant, looked in. In that
mirror he caught his eyes, though his back was to
him, and there was a peculiarly puzzled and concentrated look in them. Dick called out—

"I say, Harry—Sergeant, I mean"—it would not
do to be too familiar before the general public—
"Deuce take it! he's gone too! Why, what on
earth is the matter with them, I wonder?" This air
of mystery was really annoying.

The two friends appealed to seemed to discover
another good joke, and laughed heartily. Somehow
the private could not exactly see what they were
laughing at this time.

"Was that Sergeant Yorke?" quietly asked the
gentleman with the knicker-breeches.

"All there is meant for him," was the explicit reply,
"But you seem to know him," Dick added, somewhat
surprised.

"I have the honour of being slightly acquainted
with him," was the unconcerned reply.

Somehow his manner did not invite further inquiry
into the matter, and Dick Townley rose from the
table. He wanted to get back into the smoking-car
and have a pipe of "T. & B." "I'll bid you good
afternoon, gentlemen," he said, bowing with a certain
deference; for Dick Townley, in spite of the un-

conventionality and freedom of his ways, had no thought of being forward or forgetting his position.

"Good afternoon," echoed the two friends, pleasantly.

"Stay a minute," said the stout gentleman, holding out his cigar-case. "Try one of these cigars—you'll find them good, I think."

"Thanks very much," said Dick, choosing one. "There are so many cabbage-leaves floating about in this country that it is a treat to run across a decent cigar now and again—so very good of you."

"Not at all—delighted, I'm sure," rejoined the stout gentleman; and in another instant the youth had left the car.

"'You bet,' as they say across the lines," soliloquised Dick, with the sublime magnanimity and loftiness of youth, "that these two chaps are 'big mucky-mucks' in their own little tinpot place, wherever that may be."

He was right. But then a tract of country that in extent is about the size of Europe, is not exactly a little "tinpot place."

The private made his way to the smoking-car, where he found the sergeant and the little scout. The latter, on catching sight of him, sprang to his feet and was about to say something, when the sergeant checked him by a sudden gesture.

"Well, Dick, had a good time?" queried the sergeant, in a dry and rather significant tone of voice that unaccountably nettled and mystified the private.

"So-so, thanks," was, however, the imperturbable reply. "But, why do you ask? By the way, why didn't you come into the 'diner' that time, instead of only shoving your head inside the door and going out again?"

"Oh, I merely didn't want to intrude. But what were you gassing to them about? Favouring them with one of your little philosophical dissertations on things in general. Eh?"

Somehow Dick Townley did not like the tone his superior adopted. It nettled him strangely; for it argued there was a screw loose somewhere, and that the sergeant was cross-examining him on purpose to bring confusion upon him. But the worldly-wise youth was not the one to be taken at a disadvantage. If there was anything wrong, that was his affair. Neither the sergeant nor the scout was going to make him the butt of any joke. He shaped his answer accordingly.

"Well," said he, sitting down, putting his feet on the seat opposite, and deliberately lighting his cigar, "you see, Harry, these two chaps were somewhat dicky about their Latin. One of them—the fat one—appealed to me as to whether his way was not the right one and his companion's the wrong, in pronouncing a certain word——"

"And you——?"

"Told him flatly he was wrong, to be sure."

."Oh, you did, did you? Well, Dick, you've

enough policy to qualify you for the post of Prime
Minister one of these fine days. You're sure to get
a commission in the force, anyhow. And what did
you say to the man in the knicker-breeches ? " asked
the sergeant, with an irritating vein of sarcasm in his
voice.

"Oh, I told him he was wrong also !" was the
watchful reply. "Do you think, Harry, I am one of
those amiable nonentities that go about agreeing with
every one, when I happen to know that I am right
when others are wrong ? I don't suppose they would
have admired me any the more for having agreed
with them. They seemed pretty decent, chummy
sort of fellows. But, by the way, Dick, the one
with the knicker-breeches seemed to know you. Do
you know whom they are ? "

" Slightly," was the reply, and with a furtive look
at his comrade's face. " I've had the honour of
turning out the guard at Regina, and presenting arms
to them both on several occasions. The stout one
is the Lieutenant-Governor, Joseph Royal, of the
North-West Territories, and the other is one of
your superior officers, Lieutenant-Colonel Herchmer,
Assistant Commissioner of the North-West Mounted
Police Force. . . . Oh, I can assure you, my boy, you
were in quite respectable company ! "

There was a dead pause for a second. Harry
Yorke looked pityingly at his comrade's face, as if he
expected to see that look of self-assurance change

to one of confusion and mortification. The little scout's large, bulging black eyes fairly danced in his head, as he prepared to enjoy the expected *dénouement*. But he was to suffer disappointment. Dick Townley observed these signs as he blew a larger wreath of smoke than usual out of his mouth, and nipped, as it were, in the bud an impulse to utter a rather pronounced ejaculation. He never even once shifted in his seat, but continued the conversation as if he had heard nothing extraordinary.

"Indeed," said he calmly, and with a look of candour and simplicity. "Now I can understand what o'clock it is; for I could not quite make out what Herchmer was driving at when he said, in the course of our rather chatty conversation, that he knew my uncle, the general, in England, and he hoped that when in Regina I'd take a walk over to his diggings now and again when he'd endeavour to show me some attention. Of course, I didn't understand that he was one of my officers—the sly beggar not to refer to the fact. But, perhaps, he felt some little delicacy upon that point—some scruples regarding my feelings, or something of that sort. There's nothing like keeping in with the powers that be, Harry, you know, and you bet I'll do it."

"The devil!" muttered the amazed, and now thoroughly disgusted, Harry.

As for Pierre, the scout, his eyes fairly started out

of his head ; his under jaw dropped, and his gaze
became fixed. His "dear Richard," as he frequently
called the private, sometimes indeed astonished
him, but had never done so as much as on this
occasion.

"And Joe Royal, he's not a bad sort of fellow
either," continued Dick, as if soliloquising. "He
wanted me to stay in the car and finish another
bottle with them. But as I had already sampled
their wine and cigars pretty freely, I said I'd join
them later on in the day, and honour them with my
presence. (Doesn't do, you know, to make one's self
too cheap.) Royal said, when I asked him where
he was bound for, that he was going to Regina,
like myself." At this piece of information the sergeant groaned, and the private, asking him sharply
what the matter was with him, but receiving no
response, proceeded again, " He also expressed his
regret that he had not his card-case with him. However, I gave him my card, whereupon he expressed
the hope that I would be able to come over to dinner
at his place one of these days. He said there were
some people in the neighbourhood whom he thought
I'd like to meet."

"Oh! of course," broke in the sergeant, with a
voice so freezingly polite that it seemed to afford
the precocious youth considerable amusement, "of
course, he meant the Commissioner, the Assistant
Commissioner, perhaps the Governor-General, Hayter

Reed, the Indian Commissioner, Nicholas Flood Davin, M.P., Sir W. C. Van Horne, and a few others—like yourself, you know. Oh, fire away, Dick! I did not think it were possible for any human being to arrive at such a lofty pitch of intellectual impenetrability! Your utter lack of the perceptive faculty borders on the sublime! And you didn't seem to think it strange when he did not give you his card? Oh, no, I don't suppose you thought about that at all!"

At the bare thought of the story the two magnates would have to relate concerning his friend, the sergeant grew hot and cold by turns. He had meant to overwhelm the luckless private with a sense of shame; but here was that individual, to talk figuratively, wallowing in it, like a hog in the mire. Well, wonders would never cease.

But Dick thought the sergeant had been punished sufficiently, so turned his attention to the luckless scout to put the finishing touch, as he mentally construed it, on him.

"As for you, Pierre, the Assistant Commissioner asked what the matter was with you—that time you were making faces at me in the car, and went out so hurriedly. I am sorry if I should have done wrong, but I fear I said, to excuse your extraordinary behaviour, that you had been indulging a little too freely—indeed, to tell the truth, I said you had been on a prolonged spree, and were hardly responsible for your actions. However, as I promised Herchmer I'd look him up again to-night in the private Pulman, I'll fix it all right again for you."

Poor Pierre sat limp, the picture of apprehension (he was on his last trial), and with the cold sweat starting from him. He was unable to utter a word.

Dick Townley rose with an air of unruffled and benign composure, threw away the stump of his cigar, and went over to the bookstall to buy a book from the newsagent.

"I rather think that fetched them," said this unsophisticated and innocent youth to himself. "You see, Harry had it all his own way with that pretty girl at St. Denis' ranche—not another chap could get an innings at all; and, besides, he thought to extinguish me altogether with that wonderful news of his a minute or two ago. Pierre, also, has been getting rather cocky lately, and wanted taking down a peg. When one goes in for turning the tables, one wants to take sweeping and active measures, or else something will be recoiling and damaging one. . . . Great Scott! but now I come to think of it, I *did* tell the Assistant Commissioner when he asked me what I thought of the force 'that it wouldn't be a bad sort of outfit to be in if they could only manage to hang one or two of the officers, and put some brains into one or two of the others.' Well—I am a bright sort of bird after all!"

As he reseated himself his face wore a somewhat

thoughtful and preoccupied air. Abstractedly he whistled the Dead March in Saul in a minor key.

After all, Dick's triumph was not unlike all other earthly ones—it was not unmixed.

CHAPTER XV.

THE headquarters of the North-West Mounted Police
Force at Regina stand on a site as drearily featureless and wretched for the herding together of human
beings as ever the most interested or disinterested of
mortals fixed upon. No rolling prairie here to unfold
to the traveller every few miles some varying scene
suggestive of change, and restful to the eye and
the senses. Nothing but a dead level—a seemingly
interminable plain as far as the eye can reach. A
prairie without a tree, a stick, a stone, or a hillock
higher than an ant-hill, to break the appalling
reiteration and maddening monotony of the weary
landscape. In winter a snow-clad, wind-swept,
blizzard-haunted wilderness. In spring and summer,
when it rains, a quagmire of the most oleaginous
and tenacious mud that ever stuck to boots worn by
human beings. But this mud grows excellent wheat ;
and people, as a rule, do not emigrate merely in
search of the picturesque.

"By what strange paths and crooked ways" the town of Regina, and the North-West Mounted Police barracks came to be placed where they are, is one of those mysteries left to puzzle the student of history in the time to come. All honour, however, to the energetic inhabitants of Regina—to those who have administered its affairs, and its able Press, that they have made their city what it now is. You, in particular, Nicholas Flood Davin, and Mowat, have been men amongst thousands.

But it is the headquarters of the North-West Mounted Police Force, and not the town of Regina that we have to do with. The barracks are situated some two miles west of the town, and constitute in themselves a goodly village, with their great octagon-shaped water-tank, like a tower in the centre, flag-staff, handsome riding-school, large stables, and other buildings. They stand on the banks of the Wascana Creek—the favourite haunt and breeding-place of the festive mosquito in the spring—and upon the whole are not a particularly inspiriting sight. If rumour speaks truly—and rumour must be taken with the proverbial pinch of salt—the enterprising individual who sold this site to the police force for so much cash, and, some say, the promise of a commission in the force, had the best of the bargain.

Entering the barracks by the principal gateway one passes the great flag-staff on the right, and on the left the long, low wooden guard-room where Louis Riel, Gaudier, Racette, and other enemies to the law and their own freedom of action, enjoyed for a period the enforced hospitality of the provost-sergeant, and at last one fine morning walked out of the window at the gable end of the building to pay the penalty of their misdeeds. The rope that hanged the famous rebel Riel is one of the longest ropes on record; for Jack Henderson, the worthy Scot from the island of Bute, who hanged him, is accredited with having sold at least several miles of that same rope. After all, Jack Henderson only hanged the man who, on one occasion, came very near to hanging him. It was only right that Jack should be allowed to use a long rope.

In front of the guard-room, pacing up and down on the side-walk, between huge banks of snow, is the sentry, minus his carbine ; for it is thirty below zero, and cold steel is a dangerous thing to handle in such a low temperature. He resembles nothing so much as a huge bear, with his great shaggy buffalo coat, his capacious collar up over his ears, fur cap, and long brown stockings folded below the knee. Of course in such weather he wears no long top boots, but moccasins. On the west side of the square are two large blocks of two-storied barrack-rooms for the men. In front of No. 1 passage the sick parade has fallen in, and the orderly corporal is standing by, ready to march off the little row of unfortunates to

the doctor the minute the bugle is sounded. But to
the credit of the medical staff of the police force be
it said, they are capable of performing their duties
with marked ability and humanity.

And now, in spite of the inclemency of the weather,
the side-walks of the square are thronged with men,
hurrying backwards and forwards as if their lives
depended on it. There are two or three hundred
souls in the barracks, and what with parades of one
kind and another : rides, drills, fatigues, &c., they
have a busy time of it. Regina, generally speaking,
is the *bête noir* of the Mounted Policeman. It is the
training school he has to pass through before being
sent to one of the far and many outposts scattered
throughout the Territories.

A quarter to eleven now, and there is another little
group of men opposite " No. 1 " passage ready to fall
in before the orderly room bugle-call sounds. This
is, generally speaking, the parade of the day ; the one
round which most interest centres. For it consists of
delinquents, and their individual demeanours, under
trying and peculiar circumstances, present interesting
studies to the student of character or psychology.
How quickly one can spot the raw recruit, who with
the outwardly unconcerned face and hectic laugh, but
with that peculiarly anxious and concentrated look
in his eye betraying him, is about to go up before his
commanding officer for the first time, to be charged
with the terrible crime " in that he did allow a horse

to break away from him when leading it to water " on the previous day, or something of a like treasonable nature. Moreover, as there is no fixed scale of punishment in this force, a man who happens to be disliked by a certain officer may find himself heavily fined, or even imprisoned, when another man goes Scot free for a more serious offence. A certain able and conscientious Member of Parliament, however, a year or two ago, taught certain autocratic police officials that there was a limit to despotism in Her Majesty's service.

It needs no one to point out the old offender—there he is, cool as a cucumber, and (with a hardihood that positively fills the young recruit aforesaid with mingled consternation and awe), chaffing the orderly corporal—not yet confirmed — most unmercifully. The corporal who, upon principle, promptly suppresses any liberties taken by newcomers in the force, stands somewhat in dread of this great six-foot-three giant, who is a carpenter to trade, and is known as " Tom." Moreover, the giant is an old hand and an Irishman to boot. At every fresh sally —at the corporal's expense—the little crowd in vain endeavours to suppress the laugh that will break out. The corporal turns red, and tries to assert his dignity ; but it is of no use : Tom's wit is too subtle: so obviously free from any personal animus towards the non-com. and so good-natured withal, that reprisal is next to impossible. Suddenly Harry Yorke, the

14

sergeant, joins the little group, and comes to the
rescue of the unhappy corporal.

" Shure, now thin ye bhlaghart," he says to Tom,
imitating the brogue with a surprising exactitude,
"an' is it juist when ye will be goin' to git another tin-
dhollar foine up yere shleeve that ye will be phlaying
the goat loike this ? But what are you on the peg
this time for, Tom—another drunk ? "

" Dhivil a bhit, sarjint, dhear," answered the Irishman, with an aggrieved look on his face, so well
simulated indeed that one or two recruits who stood
looking on, and had not sufficient experience of Tom,
felt sorry for him. " Another dhrunk, indade ! And
shure if it wir another dhrunk it wud not be moindin'
the thin-dhollars up my shleeve I'm thinkin' I'll git ;
but as it is the oidentical same dhrunk I wis foined
last week for, it's phlaying it low on the carpentirs
shop I'm thinkin'. Oh wirra, wirra ! And what will
my poor ould mother say if she hears of this, at all,
at all."

At this point Tom looked such a picture of misery
that one of the very young recruits stammered out a
few broken words of sympathy. Then Tom's eyes
fairly danced in his head ; but he thanked the youthful constable politely, with a look of preternatural
gravity on his face that somewhat mystified the
others. He turned to the sergeant and continued—

" An' sarjint, darlin', what will they be goin' to

hang ye for? an' bad luck to thim by the same token as does it sez oi."

"For allowing a young woman to leave a house in which I was, during the night, Tom," was the somewhat unwise and unwilling reply of Harry Yorke.

At this Tom opened his eyes and stared at the sergeant in a manner that was meant to express astonishment, disapprobation, and a sort of pitying disparagement all in one.

"Ochone, ochone, sarjint, dhear, but it will be sarvin' ye right if they take the sthripes of yere coat for that same, shure; an' what would it be ye wir lettin' the poor crither go for—an' in the noight? An' if it had been mysilf, now, it's dhivil a fut I'd have let her go — leastways, ahlone. It's mysilf would have been comforting an' kapin' the puirty mavourneen compiny shure. Shame on ye for that same, sarjint! If Larry's got iny sinse av gallantry himsilf, he'll sock it t' ye an' no mistake, an' hair on 'im for that same sez oi."

And amid the easy laughter of old offenders, and the distressingly artificial laughter of the new, the order was given to "fall in." At the same moment two or three men rushed from the passage, and fell in with the others, Dick Townley being one of them. The men were told off by sections from the left. The order was given, "Half sections left — quick march;" and, as one man, the little band was marched half round the square by the side-walk to the adjutant's room, where the Dispenser of Justice sat in state surrounded by the other officers in the post.

To avert the by no means unlikely contingency of being frozen, they were marched into a little side-room, there to await their turns for appearing.

Then the sergeant-major gave the order, " Sergeant Yorke, and evidence—t' shun, right turn, quick march," and into the presence of the dispenser of justice, Harry Yorke, Dick Townley, and Pierre the scout were ushered. "Mark time in front—give me your cap, Sergeant Yorke. Halt, right turn," and the beginning or the end of the play had begun.

But what need to detail the phraseology of the long-winded charge that was preferred against Sergeant Yorke, or the scene that followed. There was Inspector Bounder, his round face glowing with zeal and virtuous indignation. As first witness on the evidence, he related how Sergeant Yorke had wilfully neglected the precautions he, his superior officer, had taken such pains to charge him with. And how Sergeant Yorke must have connived with that girl, Marie St. Denis—who might be, for all he knew, a girl of light character, but was at least as bad as her father, a notorious smuggler, to allow her to leave the hut surreptitiously and so cause the frustration of the ends of justice.

At this point the hands of Sergeant Yorke twitched convulsively as he stood at attention ; the veins in his forehead stood out ; he drew his breath in short

quick gasps that made every eye in the room look
at him wonderingly. There was one grey-haired,
elderly surgeon in the little group of officers, who
coughed significantly behind his hand, stared at the
inspector who was giving evidence with a look of
indignation and disgust, and then turned his back
significantly and contemptuously upon him.

Brave old Dr. Dodd, your memory is a sacred
thing with every man who had the honour of coming
in contact with you in the North-West Mounted
Police Force!

To the credit of the officer who was trying the
case be it said, he at this point pulled Inspector
Bounder pretty sharply up, telling him to confine
himself to the charge, and to be careful regarding
what aspersions he made respecting any woman.

Jamie took the snub easily enough. A man without any sense of honour can neither be insulted nor
snubbed : he is conscious of the cap fitting — the
shape of his ugly head gives him away—and he
knows that the best way of getting over the difficulty
is by taking no notice of it.

Perhaps, after all, Jamie's evidence did not do
Sergeant Yorke as much damage as it might have
done. His personal animus affected that dispassion-
ate critical sense which is necessary to work out a
logical and conclusive conviction. In his hatred of the
man before him, he evolved from his own gross and
sluggish imagination utter fabrications which he had

no means of proving, and left unnoticed points that, had they been put to the prisoner or the witnesses, might easily have been construed into neglect of duty or breaches of discipline. To say that the officer who was trying the case realised this, and felt heartily ashamed of the feeble case against the accused, were putting it mildly. The accused had no questions to ask of this witness.

Then the private, Dick Townley, was examined. His evidence only contradicted that of the previous witness.

As for the little scout, in whose simplicity and ignorance of the effects of heckling had lain the chief hope of Jamie, he showed himself at least a firm believer in one most excellent precept—"silence is golden." Moreover, he seemed to have become slow of comprehension to a degree; and what know-ledge of the Queen's English he had possessed at one time, seemed to have entirely deserted him. Outwardly he resembled the heathen Chinee, his smile being "childlike and bland," and when evi-dently unable to understand some rather pointed question that was put to him by the Dispenser of Justice, there was a puzzled and meek pensiveness upon his face that would have done credit to one of the martyrs of the Inquisition. When cautioned regarding this line of conduct in a way that would hardly have been permitted in any other orderly room save in the North - West Mounted Police

Force (where one man relegates to himself powers
that a court-martial of experienced British officers in
other parts of the Empire would hesitate to exercise),
he betrayed a most deplorable and imperfect condition of memory. He could recollect nothing. To
the student of psychology, or the investigator of
mental diseases, Pierre would have proved a most
interesting study. But this condition of mind is not
peculiar to those holding subordinate positions in the
force. Perhaps on other momentous occasions it has
proved efficacious. It is only pure speculation to say
that probably some analogous circumstance suggested
itself to the quick comprehensive mind of the stern,
but not altogether heartless officer who was trying
the case, for a twinkle shot into those somewhat rest-
less, greyish-blue eyes beneath the bushy eyebrows,
and in a quick, jerky, somewhat American-like drawl,
he ordered the scout to stand aside.

Then the question was put to the prisoner, " Well,
Sergeant Yorke, what have you got to say for
yourself ? "

It was a rather remarkable thing that the officer
trying the case should never look at the prisoner.
Perhaps it was as well. Who knows but that beneath
the almost harsh demeanour, the too strict and stern
sense of discipline that nearly always characterised
his bearing towards those whom he officially came
in contact with, there was a tender place in this man's
heart, the existence of which he was conscious of,

and which was always a menace against the proper
carrying out of an all too rigorous policy which he
erroneously considered it his duty to pursue. Doubtless he erred on the side of duty ; and true to
the adage that "extremes meet," his policy was
productive of much that militated against a healthy
moral tone, and that sense of honour it is essen-
tially necessary should prevail in a police force.
But, regarding the man himself, at heart he was
a well-meaning man ; and to any one who could
see beneath the surface of things, who could read
aright the intonation of a voice or the glance of
an eye, no matter how harsh and severe they seemed,
there was much that was good and even likable in
him. He was one of the stern sort. He doubtless
was sorry when he saw a good man come to grief,
but he never said so. Perhaps if a little of the
suaviter in modo had come more naturally to him,
he would have been more popular than he was. No
man living need think that he can rule solely by the
fortiter in re. In the natural order of things it cannot
be : the darkest tragedies of history are written in
the blood of tyrants. In justice to this man, however,
be it said that in his heart there was no hatred
towards his fellow-man ; it was a pity he should be
so afraid of that better self which was most assuredly
in him. It would not have detracted from the dignity
or power of his position. A beneficial and lasting
influence would thus have been exercised, instead of a

mistaken and pernicious species of terrorism that did a hundred times more harm than good.

And now there was a significant silence in that orderly room, and every eye was turned inquiringly on the accused. With the more than lightning-like rapidity of thought, Harry Yorke had realised the position in which he stood. He knew that as Inspector Bounder, with his usual shortsightedness, had seen no tracks of a woman's feet leading from the house-door, it would be dangerous for him to say to the Presiding Officer that he had not looked for tracks ; he—Sergeant Yorke—had therefore only to say that the girl must have escaped from her bed-room window or by some back door, and he could clear himself of the responsibility ; for the officer's commands had been given, specifically enough, to watch the kitchen door from the room in which they lay, but given only when the girl had made good her escape. But to Sergeant Yorke there was only one thing that was evident, and that was, whatever con-struction he might put upon his conduct, he could never be otherwise than guilty in his own eyes. To make a clean breast of the whole affair would be to commit a palpable absurdity that the law did not demand, that no one would thank him for, and that would not only incriminate Marie St. Denis, but would not mitigate his offence. Such a course was not to be thought of. Again, if by using that pre-rogative which wisely enough is permitted the British soldier, of making the best defence he can for himself, he utterly upset the inspector's charge— which, being wrong to begin with, could have easily been accomplished—and he proved that there was in reality no ground for a conviction against him, would it be conducive to his self-respect? The very idea of denying the fact of having aided the flight of Marie St. Denis seemed in itself the most objectionable treason. It was like denying her— she who, in spite of all that had taken place, he felt was well worthy of his respect, and who, indeed at all times, was occupying a very great share in his thoughts. Deny her, indeed!—and his denial of this charge would be akin to it—he felt it would better become him to draw attention to the base insinuation of the commissioned cad, who had, to further his own selfish ends, aspersed the fair name of a pure-minded girl. Deny the charge, indeed! and God-given thought suggested to him that old-world scene, where in the court of the High Priest's palace a fond but faint-hearted follower stood warming himself in the chill dawn by a fire of coals, but whose love, alas! was not proof against that significant soul-searching question, " Did I not see thee in the garden with him ? " For the answer came back with an oath, " I know not the man ! " as he denied the master. What more simple or comprehensive in this world's history than such a lesson ? How could he again look that girl in the face, knowing that he had lied to save three paltry stripes? There was sin enough against him as it was. Now that a nobler ideal had come into his life—the thought of that sacrifice of a girl's pride (what man can measure it?) to save an erring father, be it right or wrong in its object—made him feel that it would be dishonourable to her, and in him, to deny the charge now. The knowledge that he would voluntarily quit that calling he had chosen in a few weeks, because he felt himself no longer worthy of it, was not sufficient to bias his judgment. In a second his resolve was taken. He would apply and profit by the old-world story, and no ironical cock would bear witness to his denial. In another second he said—

" I have nothing to say in my defence ; but perhaps Inspector Bounder would like an opportunity of explaining what he meant by referring to Miss St. Denis as he did."

Had he given voice to some treasonable utterance he could not have surprised the little group of officers standing round their chief more than he did. As for the latter, man of action and quick-witted as he was, he was momentarily taken aback. The sergeant-major, who stood behind the prisoner, breathed quickly. He did not know whether it was his duty to silence this outspoken offender or not. But the chief looked up quickly, and to his credit said—

" You have no right to demand an explanation

from Inspector Bounder—that is my business, and you can rest assured I shall do so."

Then he hesitated a moment, with pen in hand, ere he wrote on the back of the defaulter sheet. This done he said, still in that quick, jerky way—

"You have not a clean defaulter sheet" (it took a very clever man or a nonentity to keep a clean sheet in the police force), "but this is the first charge reflecting on your honour that has been brought against you. Such a charge wants making an example of. One month's pay" (enough to bury three policemen), "and reduced to the rank and pay of a constable."

"Left turn, quick march," rang out the stentorian voice of the sergeant-major; and in another minute *Private* Yorke and evidence stood outside.

"I've a knife in my pocket, sergeant-major," said Private Yorke as he held up his right sleeve to that officer.

In another minute the three golden bars and the crown were being ripped off his serge. "I'm very sorry for you, Yorke, old man," whispered the sergeant-major. "Come and see me when orderly room is over."

He was a good-hearted fellow the sergeant-major and had "been there" himself in his time.

CHAPTER XVI.

SOME LIVES FROM THE RANKS.

HARRY, old man," said Dick Townley, as he caught his comrade by the arm, and walked along the sidewalk with him, "it's no use telling you how sorry I am for you ; you must know all that. You'll have your stripes back again before long, depend on it. In the meantime I'll give you a hand to shift your things from your old quarters. You must come into No. 9 room ; there's a place for a set of trestles and boards alongside mine. There's no corporal in the room. You will be in charge anyhow, and won't have to do room-orderly."

" Thanks, Dick," said Private Yorke, trying to look cheerfully upon the prospect before him, and not quite succeeding. " Don't think for a moment I'm going to break my heart, lad. I got these stripes "— he carried them in his hand now—" for my share in catching Blueblanket's son, and it does seem a little hard to have to chuck them up like this. But I've only a month or so to put in, and then I'm a free nigger. But, I guess, I'll pan out somehow. There's the C. P. R., the Hudson Bay Company, or perhaps I may go on my own hook. I've a few thousand dollars, thank goodness. The first move will want the most consideration."

Then somehow he thought of Marie St. Denis. After all, he had been loyal to himself and to her. If he had erred he was now voluntarily paying the penalty of his error. He had not surrendered his self-respect by equivocating and escaping that penalty. He had been true to her in his heart; he somehow felt as if he had suffered for her. Already there seemed a subtle bond of union between them. His spirits rose. He felt as if somehow Marie St. Denis were nearer to him—at least, he had taken one step towards her. After all, if he had lost the stripes he felt something else within him—something that made him feel as if he had a better title to the name of a man, than all the stripes and gold lace in the police force in themselves could possibly have given him. "*Broke!*" It was an ugly word, truly, but he could afford to smile at it now.

And then he looked down at the bare place on his coat-sleeve where the stripes had been ; his eye had instinctively missed them. "Damn the stripes and those who took them from me !" he broke out. He could hardly be expected to take to his new position all at once.

Perhaps what affected him more than anything

was the spontaneous, delicate, and heart-felt expressions of sympathy when he reached the men's quarters
from non-coms., and privates alike. They pressed
forward one after another, and shook him warmly by
the hand. "Never mind, Yorke," said one, "you're
too good a man to vegetate as a sergeant. If you
take the stripes again—and they'll be running after
you again to take them in a few weeks—we'll cut
you dead." "Yorkey," said another, "it may be
questionable taste in expressing myself as I do, but
we, one and all, are proud and glad to have you
amongst us again." A drill instructor, a fair-haired,
smart, soldierly-looking man, actually had told the
little squad of men he was drilling in an adjoining
room to "stand easy" and made his way over to
Harry. "Old-hand" that he was, he could see almost
without appearing to look that the three stripes
and crown had disappeared from his coat-sleeve.
There were four stripes on his own coat. His style
of administering comfort was, perhaps, the best of
any. As he pressed Harry's hand he said with a
pleasant, careless smile on his face, "What's the
odds, Yorke! You know enough about this force to
take such an ordinary everyday occurrence for what
it's worth. Was it the Psalmist, or some other chap
who said, 'Man is born unto troubles as the sparks
fly upwards,' or something of that sort? If the
Psalmist—with all due deference to him—had been
a North-West Mounted Policeman, he might have

put the case a little more strongly, and said, ' There is nothing certain to the unbeliever save a comprehensive defaulter sheet, and an enforced period of entertainment in Trigot's hotel.'   So far as non-coms. are concerned, not one of us is sure of his stripes for twelve hours."

He was right; within the week he was on his way up to Prince Albert minus his four stripes, and taking his orders from a French Canadian teamster who happened to be his senior.   He proved the truth of his words, anyhow.   Harry Yorke had hardly taken a survey of the spot, where he contemplated taking his boards and trestles to, in No. 9 barrack-room, when a prisoner's escort entered the room with side-arms on, in charge of Tom the Hibernian carpenter.

" Hilloa, Tom, what did you get ? " some one cried, as he observed the luckless one proceed to bundle up his kit as if preparing for a removal !

"What did I git ? " was¡ the somewhat rueful answer, " why, I got it socked to me, shure !   Bad luck to Larry, the blood-thirsty ould coyote, it's doin' a month he should be himsilf.   Shure now, wouldn't I like to be following the ould sinner round the square wid me baton, an' him carrying round the coals to the officers' quharters.   Holy mother av Moses if I wouldn't make him git a rustle on !   Yis bhoys, ould Joey's got mi now."

And here Tom paused in the task of rolling up his bedding, to sing for the benefit of the company a

popular ditty that had been composed by a guard-
room poet, in reference to the relationship in which,
generally speaking, sooner or later the provost-
sergeant, otherwise head-gaoler—known as Joey—
stood to the young tenderfoot who had committed
some trifling error.   The chorus of the song, in which
two or three of the men joined, ran thus :—

> " For old Joey's got him now,
>   And the sweat's on his beautiful brow ;
>   Going round from house to house,
>   Clad in a coloured blouse,
>   Old Joey's got him now."

It is only justice to the Joey referred to, however,
to say that his bark was worse than his bite.   If his
manner was at times rather harsh, he never allowed
a poor civilian prisoner to leave his charge on the
expiry of his sentence, without a heartfelt " Get out
of this and don't come here again ! "—and a dollar in
his pocket.

It was a unique scene—one which could hardly
have been witnessed outside a North-West Mounted
Police barrack-room, where, generally speaking, the
men pull well together.   There was an ex-sergeant—
Harry Yorke—assisting a prisoner who had just got,
as he expressed it, " thirty days in the hotil," and
every one present joining in a serio-comic chorus,
with the exception of the extremely youthful prisoner's
escort, who was scared within an inch of his life by the
prisoner he was in charge of, and kept wondering if a

plug of tobacco would assist in conciliating the terrible
Irishman.

"Shure an' it's no use av mi sympathisin' wid
you, Sarjint—I mane Corpiril. Oh—damn what I
mane anyhow, Sarjint Yorke. Oh, Jerusalem!—for
I'm in a worse box moisilf than you. But niver
moind 'we shall meet on that be-autiful shore' as
my dear frind Pat Barnes over in Joey's says. An' I
say, Sarjint Yorke,—dhivil take stroipes anyway—it's
likely you'll be hevin' your turn at escort in a day or
two and there's five dollars I want ye to kape for me.
Two plugs av 'T. an' B.' a wake, me bhoy! The
two assistant provosts are demned dacent lads, one
an owd guardsman and another an ould mossback, an'
may be dipended on to trate me discrately. My
blessin' on ye bhoys an be good to your silves."

And Tom, the carpenter, with a roll of bedding
on his back (for use in the guard-room) took his
depàrture from No. 9 barrack-room, and out of this
history.

That night in "No. 9 barrack-room" there was
one man at least who lay awake long after "lights-
out," and indulged in many long and anxious
thoughts. Last night he was lying the sole occupant
of the room at the end of the passage, sergeant in
charge of the four barrack-rooms that it commanded.
To-night—well, he had been warned for stable-orderly
on the morrow, and that explained the situation.
After all, it served him right: a man of his experience

of the world, and education, to join a police force,
because there were many more "had-beens" like
himself in it ; and where, to keep up the delusion of
playing at soldiers, they fined and imprisoned till the
red coat of a British dragoon was a mockery to a
man. He was in a bitter and cynical mood. He
began to feel that passion and not reason was swaying
him now. Let him only bethink himself. Did he
not deserve the punishment he had brought upon
himself? Some voice within him said, it was for
a helpless woman's sake. But in the name of all
that was reasonable, what right had he to subvert
the law, which he represented in his person, for a
matter of sentiment, no matter how just and reasonable he might think it ? If he had erred in a matter
of judgment, he ought to have known that the path
of duty was a straight one, permitting of no turning
either to the right or the left, and he ought to have
followed it. When he came to think of it, his punishment was only just ; moreover, he himself had courted
that same punishment. He had no reason to find
fault with the powers that had tried him. They had
even, perhaps, dealt leniently with him.

But was it not an ill luck that was for ever dogging
his steps ? He sat up in his bed now, as if to relieve
the rush of blood that had gone to his fevered head.

Luck, forsooth ! Who was he that he should talk
of luck ? Let him glance around where stretched
upon their palliasses lay the slumbering forms of his

comrades, and let him just take one by one the life
histories—at least, so much as was known of them—
of these men : a fair sample of some of the pathetic
and almost tragic histories that were buried away in
this police force.

There, within a couple of yards of him, lay one
who was in his day one of the most famous and
promising men in his university. He had rowed in
the eight ; he had been a Senior Wrangler ; he had
taken the highest honours wherever he had essayed to
conquer in the paths of knowledge ; he had entered
the church ; a man of great heart and brain whom
every one was proud to know. Surely his was a life
to be envied and emulated : surely his life was a
success. And then—what was that awful thing—
that evil genius, that reptile-like had followed him
up with pitiless malignity—stealing upon him again
with redoubled rigour after every fresh repulse, and
then striking with its deadly, pitiless fangs when it
was sure of its victim ? *Drink !* disgrace—ruin—ay,
something infinitely worse than death ! And then—
another name—another and a new country ; the red
coat of the dragoon as worn by a Mounted Police
force—for he could not rid himself of that life which
had become a burden to him ; he was too much of
a man to cut it short with his own hands. Then
he had turned over a new leaf, and was about to
get the promotion that his abilities had earned for
him—but he had fallen again. Only that day he had

come out of the guard-room where he had been performing a prisoner's menial tasks.   What was to be
the end of him?   Oh, the ironies of what man calls
fate !

And there, in that other cot, with a ghostly ray of
moonlight creeping over the old brown rug, lay
another " had-been."   At one time the most popular
officer in a crack cavalry old-country regiment : a
man who had the respect of his brother officers and
the love and confidence of the rank and file ; a man
of supposed large private means and influence ; for
whom there were great things in store, and who had,
figuratively speaking, the ball at his foot.   And then
—talk of it shudderingly, and with bated breath—
was it something at cards? or did rumour lie?   Be
it as it might, he had dropped out of that distinguished life as completely as if his charger had been
led riderless, with boots reversed, on the soldier's
last parade, and a volley of musketry had been discharged over his grave.   There were some who said
it had been better so.   What availed now his medals
and clasps for distinguished service?   He durst not
wear them, lest his story might get about.   Perhaps
only Dick and one or two others knew his melancholy history, and they kept it a sacred secret.   They
strove in pity to help this man who had erred, not
because he had once been "somebody," but because
he had been punished for his sins and was himself
striving to lead a new life.

There in that other cot in the corner, deep in shadow, lay the only son of a widowed mother, who with him had been left penniless by some sudden and unexpected monetary crisis. Brought up to a life of ease and plenty, he found that gifts like his had little chance of earning salt in a country like England, where the race was only for the strong and the trained. He had emigrated to Canada. But those who employed him—only manual labour of the most unskilled and menial sort could he get—had after a brief trial of him dispensed with his services. They said that, no matter however willing a man might be, the hands of a woman and the lack of bodily strength and ordinary skill would not suit them. Then from one stage of hardship and penury to another; and then, nothing between him and starvation but the red coat. Yes, here at last was a life where intelligence and a knowledge of horses and fire-arms would stand him in stead. And now he had taken the position of servant to an officer, in order that the extra five dollars a month which he earned by it might swell the little sum that every month, with religious punctuality, he sent home to his mother and sisters in the Old Country. Nor did he stop here, but blacked the boots of many of his comrades—many of whom had some little private means—so that he might make an extra ten or fifteen cents by doing so. Think of it—a graduate of one of the English universities, blacking boots and flunkeying for those who,

in comparison with him, belonged to a lower order of
beings altogether, so that he might send an extra ten
cents to a widowed mother. Noble life ! though only
a matter of duty some may say. Nobility and boot-
blacking, oh, ye gods ! Yes, my masters—ten thousand times *Yes !*—and nobility of a very much higher
order than any that can be granted by royal letters
patent.

Oh, the undreamt-of tragedies ! oh, the pathos
contained in the histories of some of those lives
hidden away under the scarlet tunic of the dragoon !
Those lives, the greater number of which were more
wonderful romances than any ever penned by the
hand of man, and which were now bound together by
a something more than the merely conventional term
of *camaraderie*—by a spirit of sympathy and common
brotherhood. Oh, the infinite and unspeakable possibilities of human life ! But beyond the veil, and
guiding as it were the finger of what men call Destiny,
was there no existent great and just power that
appealed to the mind and the faith of those tried
ones, helping them to do what the spirit of religion
demanded of them—which was to crush down the
devil in them that would fain rob them of their
ultimate reward ?

A few minutes before, Yorke had given way to
this demon of discontent and revolt with the insidious
whisperings. But he had thought of the lives of these
men who lay side by side with him. These lives

which were not the outcome of a puling and sickly
sentimentality, such as is affected by the drawing-
room scribe who has never seen life outside that
congenial apartment, but lives in the rough, the
lives of strong men with noble aspirations and strong
passions—at the very doors of whose hearts the very
muse of Tragedy herself had knocked.   What were
his troubles compared with theirs, indeed ? And what
was this life but a trial of faith after all ? . . . Truly,
no fight no victory.

He rose from his cot, and going down on his knees
did what he had neglected to do for many a long
year—he prayed.   He was not the first man who had
done so in a barrack-room ; and, perhaps, there were
those near him who had a share in his prayers.

A man's prayers are always answered, if only—as
they always do—they make him a better man.

CHAPTER XVII.

OVERHEARD BY THE OLD CROW.

SUMMER in New England—a quaint old farm-house with straggling outbuildings hiding amid a wealth of rustling, sweet-smelling greenery, and an air of peace and healthful existence everywhere. It was quite a patriarchal place for a new country; for Gabriel St. Denis had bought it from the representa-tives of the old Shaker whose forefathers had owned and tilled the farm for over a hundred years before him. It was a one-storied, roomy, but very erratic house; for a room had been added to the main building from time to time, probably as the demand for space of some growing family had necessitated, until it was impossible to tell which of the many sides of the house constituted the front and which the back. There was nothing to guide one in deter-mining this point, for there were three different porches to it, each one with a good deal of old-fashioned trellis work, and a profusion of roses and honeysuckle sprawling all over it. Each of these

three porches in their particular day had indicated
the front proper of the house. "The times change,
and we change with them," would have been an
appropriate motto above each doorway. Perhaps it
was the non-existence of that damp, bare, stained,
slip-shod, untidy side to this house, and commonly
called " the back," that contributed to the mystery.
There were beautiful roses trained against the walls
everywhere, and flower-pots with geraniums and
fuchsias in them on the window-sills. Some people
have got an idea that you cannot see a real picture of
rural beauty outside the Old Country, but then some
people never travel. To admire another place need
not be to detract from the beauty of a home picture.
That would be an impossibility.

In the bright and pleasant sitting-room by the
open window a girl sat sewing a button on a shirt.
Now there is not much poetry in a shirt-button of
itself; but when a pretty girl is sewing one on, it
becomes quite another thing. Therefore the button
and the shirt were quite in keeping with the idyllic
surroundings. The girl's head was mostly somewhat
inclined over her work ; but from time to time she
lifted it, to smile at some caustic and original remark
that the elderly, dark-skinned woman, who was
folding some snowy linen and stowing it away in a
little sideboard, was addressing to her. But, upon
the whole, the girl, who was Marie St. Denis, did
not seem to take that interest in her self-imposed

task that she ought to have done ; neither did the
volatile and cheerful remarks of Jeannette seem to
arouse any responsive flow of spirits in her ; her
thoughts were evidently otherwise engaged. The
girl looked at some of the familiar objects of the old
Canadian days that were ranged around her, with taste
and simplicity, on the walls of that low-roofed room
—the miniature bark canoes, the tiny snowshoes, the
plumed and beaded tomahawks, the many beautiful
and delicate articles of the Indian's and half-breed's
skill in beadwork (though perhaps savouring not a
little of that barbaric richness of colouring that
the savage loves), the antique coarse blue delf that
came from France two hundred years before, the
picturesque spinning-wheel in the corner, and the
many old-world things that would have delighted the
heart of a lover of bric-a-brac. But, still, all these
familiar things did not seem to bring any sense of
comfort to her.

At last Marie threw down the shirt on which she
had sewn the refractory button, gave a little half-
querulous sigh as if of relief, and said—

" Do you know, Jeannette, I don't believe it is in
the nature of any human being to be ever really
happy. When we were upon the prairies in Assiniboia I used to think that if ever I could get dad to
come away to where there was some sort of civilisation, and to different scenes and associations—such
as these for instance, I could be quite happy, and

now that I have had my wish, that he is happy, and
even more prosperous than he was on the ranche,
there are times when everything tires and wearies me
until I could almost wish I were back again on
Many-Berries Creek."

As she spoke the roses stirred and nodded their
heads at the open window as if in assent ; there was
a subdued and drowsy murmur as of myriads of busy
bees among the honeysuckle and flowers of the old-
fashioned garden ; there was a scurry and chase of
squirrels and chipmuncks across the stem of a great
fallen tree that was used as a garden seat at the far
and shady end of the lawn ; and a hawk flew past
screeching, followed and tormented by an avenging
crowd of small birds. A butterfly fluttered in through
the open window with all the colours of the rainbow
glorifying its wings ; and the spirit of that beautiful
summer's day seemed to speak through and permeate
every living thing. Surely here if anywhere one
ought to have been happy. But it is a great mistake
that modern philosophers make when they think that
it is one's physical surroundings that conduce to
happiness—it is in one's relations and associations
with humanity that one is happy or otherwise. The
silence of the country is the worst place in the world
for a man or woman who has something to live down.
The human heart and its promptings are at all times
more potent than the mere senses ; and it is only in
work and in mixing with the busy crowd that we can

ever hope to escape for a brief space from our own rebellious selves. Human nature is, generally speaking, a complex and inexplicable thing ; but perhaps it was not so very strange, after all, that when Marie St. Denis had left Canadian Territory with all its troubled memories behind, the heart-whole, happy and careless light that used to dance in her eyes seemed to have been left behind also. There was a subtle change in her ; and what it exactly was she herself, perhaps, only imperfectly knew.

Suddenly old Jeannette turned to her, and, as if she had read the girl's thoughts, said in a quiet, kindly voice—

" Don't fret, Marie. If he is worth having he will come back for you, child. If he does not come, then, you are well rid of him : he is not worth having, and the best thing you can do is to forget. Those troopers are much alike, what I have seen of them."

This was what Jeannette had been trying to find courage to say for several weeks, and now that she had said it she was apprehensive of the consequences.

" Jeannette ! " cried the girl, imploringly, the warm blood suffusing her soft, clear skin. " You talk as if I had taken you into my confidence, and as if I had not anything else to think about. You talk as if he —for it would be nonsense to pretend I did not know whom you meant—had been a—a sweetheart, or lover, or something of that sort. Why, he never once hinted at—at the sort of thing you mean. He never acted differently towards me, more than any stranger would: only that he behaved in a very friendly manner on one occasion. I often wish now that I had cut my tongue out instead of asking a favour; for I believe it cost him his position. The thought of it sometimes drives me almost mad."

And as if she could trust herself no further, she rose and turned her back, so that Jeannette could not see her face.

" It's nothing to be ashamed of, honey; I've been thar myself," said Jeannette, smiling sadly as she thought of it. Then, with the persistent inconsistency of some good-hearted women, she went on—" But I think, Marie, he'll come back, if I am a judge of men at all. I liked his face: it was an honest one. If I have not read many books I have all my life been learning to read faces, and in his——"

But the girl had fled. She had caught up her light straw hat, and with eyes that were strangely dry and bright, and cheeks that were strangely flushed, she had run from the picturesque homestead, along the soft green turf that fringed the public road, and under the shady limes and chestnuts. She avoided the shady pasture field into which her father was helping the manservant to drive some cattle. She walked on till she came to a little rise, and then she sat down on the grass.

What was this that had changed the current of her life so, that came into her thoughts the first thing in the morning, that followed her about like a shadow all day, and that coloured her dreams at night? What was this thing that had robbed her of her girlish peace of mind, and left her heartstrings quivering and vibrating as if they had been rudely touched by some master hand? What was this thing that now seemed to her like a blessing, and now like a curse? What need to ask when it comes to nearly every one sometime or other, and there is no power on earth better known? It is that which makes or mars our lives, that which is older than the hills—they change—and is the primary and most potent instinct of our beings; it is that which makes fools of philosopher and sage, and makes fools divine; it is that which is graven on the heart of Time, can blossom from the very dust of death, and is the keynote of existence.

The girl looked down the long, dusty, and tree-fringed road, which with many a dip and gentle rise went straight on to the nearest railroad town, some four miles away. She could see a figure come travelling along slowly, about a mile or so off. Now it was on the top of a little rise, and a tiny speck it seemed, no bigger than a fly, and then it was lost to sight in one of the hollows; but always it was coming nearer and nearer.

Strange that Marie should take any interest in watching a speck! But how often had she built up castles in the air regarding those tiny specks that

came toiling along, and as they bore in sight
generally resolved themselves into importunate
tramps, or even individuals of the opposite sex
—women! She had often, for the sake of indulging
for a few brief minutes in fond expectant hope,
tortured and disappointed herself sadly, and she had
time and again resolved that she would do so no
more. But, perhaps, she did not know the strength
and persistent nature of that thing which had taken
possession of her, for day after day her footsteps had
mechanically sought that road, and her eyes had
wandered wistfully along it.

And now the solitary figure of the traveller was
lost to sight, and again it appeared on the crest of
the rising ground. No sooner there than it shortened
and disappeared again. A flock of dusty and noisy
small birds indulged in a dust-bath within a few feet
of her in the roadway. An old crow perched on a
dead limb right above her (query—why do crows
prefer dead limbs?), and who, by the way he
carried his head on one side, looked as if he knew
a thing or two, shut one eye in a critical fashion,
and looked down upon her inquiringly. He was
an inquisitive old crow: he had followed the girl
right up the road to see or hear what was going on.
It is sometimes just as well, perhaps, that crows can
only talk in their own language, otherwise the amount
of scandal that would be floating about the world
would be something horrible to contemplate. It is

a mistake to suppose that gossip and scandal are confined to the human race. Those who have lived lonely lives in the bush or on the prairie, and have had exceptional opportunities for observing, can testify to the fact that certain kinds of birds are the most persistent chatterboxes in the world. Then the girl heard a hurried pattering behind her, and Michelle, the great hound, came scampering up. It fawned upon her, and gambolled with awkward movements round her. "Poor Michelle," she said, patting the dog on the head; "*he* liked you. You never used to growl at him or be jealous of him, did you?"

Suddenly the dog lifted its head, turned round, sniffed the air, looked along the road inquiringly, and then ran a few paces forward and stopped. Dogs have a wonderfully sympathetic sense.

Then the girl's heart seemed to stand still; then to start beating so violently that she placed one hand upon her breast. Her limbs trembled under her. She stared apprehensively at the approaching figure. There was a something that obscured her vision, for the blood at first had rushed to her heart, leaving her deadly pale, then had rushed to her head, making everything, as it were, swim before her eyes, and her heart to throb almost painfully. Had the end of the world come—or the beginning? And now she saw the figure was that of a tall, dark individual with the stride of a cavalryman, who carries his toes slightly turned inwards, as if there were spurs on his heels. He was dressed in ordinary civilian clothes.

The old crow on the rotten limb, whose attention had begun to wander, roused himself all of a sudden, and gave a significant and expectant croak.

Then the stranger lifted his hat from his forehead and said—

" Miss St. Denis, don't you remember me?"

The dog crept towards him, sniffed at him, and did not growl suspiciously as was his wont at strangers, then dashed at him with boisterous welcome.

"Down, Michelle! What *are* you doing?" Marie cried to the dog, as if it were a relief to her to say something. But it was a moment or two before she could find her voice to talk to the stranger. There was a wistful, hungry look in his eyes all the while. He looked like one who was only controlling himself by a strong effort. Then she turned to him, and said in the most matter-of-fact way in the world—

" How do you do, Mr. Yorke? This is indeed a surprise. Who would have thought of seeing you in this part of the world?"

She was wonderfully self-possessed now this girl, so much so, indeed, that perhaps it was hardly natural. A stranger would have been puzzled just then to have guessed in what relationship these two stood to each other.

Even the old crow looked puzzled for a second or two. He knew that all men were liars in a more or less polished or brutal way, but that this pretty slip of a girl should have reduced it to a fine art fairly staggered him. No wonder he was a cynical old crow.

"I have just been wondering for some months back if you would be surprised to see me again," he answered slowly, and somewhat irrelevantly, watching the girl's face intently, as if he would have liked to have drawn some inference from it. "I hope you are glad to see me?" he added.

"Oh, of course," she rejoined quickly, as if she thought that perhaps she had not been quite so civil to him as she might have been ; "and my father will be glad to see an old friend, for you know you were one to him."

The hound made another circular bound into the roadway, and scattered the little birds right and left. As for the old crow, he leant back on his perch until he was in imminent danger of falling off backwards, and chuckled hoarsely and grimly to himself, as if he were immensely tickled over something. He looked as if he thanked—goodness knows what—that he was a crow and not a stupid human being. He was a satirical old crow, and looked as if he had indeed seen life. An apoplectic seizure after hearing some spicier piece of scandal than usual shall one day be his ultimate fate. Pessimists and cynics and such-

minded creatures as this crow, by the way, are
generally those who have not only—if the truth
could only be brought home to them—run the gamut
of earthly pleasures, but by violating Nature's laws
have destroyed their capacity for further enjoyment :
it is worse than a dog-in-the-manger spirit. But
perhaps this particular old crow was not quite so bad
as some of his kind.

"Marie"—the girl looked up and started slightly
as she heard him pronounce her name—"is this all
you have to say to me ? is this all the welcome you
have for me ? "

The old crow became impatient and scratched his
head vigorously with one foot.

"We might shake hands," she suggested, calmly,
but with her breath coming quickly and with
heightened colour in her cheeks.

She held out one hand to him timidly, but he
caught both of hers—and held them.

"Ha—a, ha—a !" cawed the old reprobate up on the
dead limb. Then he broke into a hoarse laugh, but
pulled himself up short, and tried to look as if he
had only been clearing his throat. He wanted to see
the whole of the comedy.

Harry Yorke looked steadily into her eyes, and.
she in turn looked shyly into his as he held her in
front of him.

"Marie," he said again, after an awkward pause,
" do you know what has brought me here ? "

"Why—why do you ask me this?" she asked, evasively; but she was shaking like a leaf, and her eyes were fixed on the ground before her.

"Because I wanted to tell you that *you* have," was the answer. "I want you to tell me that I have not done wrong in coming, and that you are glad to see me."

"Don't you think you are asking me to undertake a rather heavy contract?" she rejoined, the perverse and inscrutable promptings of old Mother Eve and the instincts of her better self each having their share in the framing and significance of this question.

"Heavy!" he repeated, somewhat taken aback, and a sudden sense of fear seizing him. "Is it, then, such a very hard thing to do?"

"But is it necessary to do it?" she persisted, ignoring his question.

"What do you mean?" he asked, fearfully, still impenetrable to the drift of her protest. There is no more stupid creature under the sun than a man when he is in love. "What is it you imply?"

"That you are like Thomas—of little faith," was the comment, with unruffled severity, "since you think it necessary to probe an old wound and view the print of the nails. Is there not *anything* you can take on trust?"

The old crow on the rotten limb lost patience with the short-sighted male animal at this point, and swore at him in a way that only a crow or a Queensland

bullock-driver can.   He had a sense of the fitness of
things at times, this old crow.

But when she lifted her eyes from the ground and
looked into his he understood her.   He drew her to
him after the manner of lovers from time immemorial
and kissed her.   " I thought you would come back to
me," she cried, in a broken voice.   There was nothing
enigmatical in her talk now ; had there been, the way
she kissed him on the lips would have explained
matters.

They lingered there so long — as lovers will
linger — holding each other's hands, and talking
about such trivial things in such tragical tones
—the usual things, the usual tones—that Michelle,
the hound, grew disgusted at the want of attention
paid him, and trotted off home with his tail between
his legs.   The sun had disappeared over the tree-tops
when these two happy ones wandered back to the
farm-house hand in hand, to have a talk with Gabriel,
and to confirm Jeannette in her belief that she was a
prophet.

As for the old crow, who was in no particular hurry
home—he belonged to the Order of the Latchkey—
he chattered and chuckled to himself in a most out-
rageous fashion ; rolled his head about till he became
giddy ; made matters worse by trying to stand
rakishly on one leg, and nearly fell off his perch ;
swore so terribly at this that he choked, gasped for
breath, and recovered ; got struck with a new idea ;

winked, but kept closing both eyes at once ; leered horribly instead, and generally misconducted himself after the manner of elderly crows who have led a fast life.   Old crows are ten times worse than young ones.   Then he flew off to retail his own version of the affair to his own particular cronies—mostly like himself—at his own particular club.   Crows are such inveterate gossips.

THE END.

www.ingramcontent.com/pod-product-compliance
Lightning Source LLC
Chambersburg PA
CBHW030404270326
41926CB00009B/1256